Project-Based Inquiry
Units for Young
Children

*First Steps to Research for
Grades Pre-K– 2*

Colleen MacDonell

**Linworth
Books**

**Professional Development Resources for
K-12 Library Media and Technology Specialists**

For Dom, as always

Library of Congress Cataloging-in-Publication Data

MacDonell, Colleen.
  Project-based inquiry units for young children : first steps to research
for grades pre-K-2 / Colleen MacDonell.
      p. cm.
  Includes bibliographical references and index.
  ISBN 1-58683-217-4 (pbk.)
  1. Project method in teaching--Handbooks, manuals, etc. 2. Inquiry-based
learning. 3. Early childhood education. I. Title.
  LB1027.43.M333 2007
  372.13'6--dc22
                                    2006021288

Published by Linworth Publishing, Inc.
480 East Wilson Bridge Road, Suite L
Worthington, Ohio 43085

ISBN: 1-58683-217-4

5 4 3 2 1

Table of Contents

Table of Contents *continued*

Table of Contents *continued*

Table of Contents *continued*

Table of Contents *continued*

Table of Figures

About the Author

Colleen MacDonell is Head Librarian at a large American-run international school. She supervises library programs for two preschools, two elementary schools, a middle school, and a high school. She holds a B.A. and M.A. in English literature, plus an education diploma and M.L.I.S. She has taught college courses on a wide variety of library science topics, including children's literature and school libraries. MacDonell is a frequent presenter at international library conferences and educational workshops. She is currently the Director for International Schools for IASL.

Acknowledgments

I would like to thank my project manager, Sherry York, for her clear and practical advice. Thanks to my husband, Dominic Larkin, for his patience and encouragement.

Introduction

Children need and desire information about the world they live in. Stories are not enough. *I Spy* books, science books about sharks or spiders, books about trucks or building a house – even books about being a gym teacher or a school librarian – can make motivating reading for young children, even when all they are "reading" are the photos or drawings or charts.

These books are not just of interest to children – informational text will later become the focus of their classroom education in elementary, middle, and high school. Strategies for building meaning from informational texts differ significantly from approaches that help children to understand and explore stories. For these reasons, early childhood educators believe it is important to expose young children to nonfiction.

Very young children can construct meaning from informational texts, but to achieve success, educators must use approaches and standards that differ from those used with older children. Books addressing the question of inquiry-based learning give few examples of how the research process works with very young children who are, at best, emergent readers. This book will show you how to lead young children from questions to answers in a meaningful way, based on the best of current research and the author's hands-on experience of what works in school library programs for children aged three through eight.

The purpose of this book is to show teachers and librarians how stories and informational texts can be used to promote research and inquiry in the earliest years of education. Set in the wider context of the project approach to learning, this book addresses the needs of both librarians and teachers in preschool, kindergarten, and primary grades. The units presented are grounded in current educational theory and the latest understanding of what is developmentally appropriate practice. Appropriate content, learning goals, and approaches to teaching and assessment are included. Examples of how early learning standards can be incorporated into projects are provided.

This book is aimed at librarians and teachers who are interested in using stories and nonfiction for their informational value. These early activities in inquiry and research are designed to be motivating to young children. Teachers and specialists are seen as partners in developing an integrated approach to student learning that is based on collaboration across subject areas and specializations. This emphasis on collaboration benefits children in that they can explore topics of interest to them in a more in-depth way, and over a longer period of time, than individual classroom lessons would allow for.

Chapter 1 looks at contemporary issues and current approaches in early childhood education. Key components of appropriate practice are covered: what content is suitable for young children, how learning goals are defined, what methodologies have a proven track record, and what defines a good classroom environment. While general guidelines about practices are widely agreed upon and supported by ongoing research, many educators and researchers in this field underscore the need for caution when devising and applying standards at this early level. Several examples of early learning standards that address these concerns well are examined. The chapter concludes with a description of the project approach to learning and its benefits for young children.

Chapter 2 moves from theory into practice with a discussion of how information texts can be used with early and emergent readers. Dialogic readings of both stories and nonfiction are dealt with in some detail. The practical tips and guidelines covered in this chapter are essential reading before tackling the projects described in the chapters that follow. A brief statement about online sources of information and assessment concludes this chapter.

Practical, hands-on activities are featured in chapters three through seven. Each chapter begins with a look at the general characteristics of a particular age group, starting with the preschool years (ages three to four) and concluding with a chapter on grade two (ages seven to eight). This general overview is illustrated with anecdotal evidence based on the author's work as a teacher and library media specialist. The overview is followed by specific strategies for helping children to deal with informational texts. Each chapter provides one detailed project description and three short project overviews. Examples of learning standards are included with the lengthier project descriptions. All projects have resource lists of stories, nonfiction, songs, fingerplays, poems, and video recordings related to the theme. Specific text strategies and teaching strategies are referred to throughout the chapters.

A list of works cited and an index conclude the book.

Chapter One

Current Research and Approaches

The Need for Quality Early Childhood Education

Improved School Readiness

Current research tells us that the early years are crucial to future success in school and career. We know that high-quality preschool programs can give disadvantaged children the help they need to succeed in elementary school and beyond(Ferrandino and Tirozzi). This is why programs like Head Start have received funding since the mid-1960s. Now more and more educators are becoming aware of new research into the importance of intervention for children from economically advantaged backgrounds as well. The National Institute of Early Education Research (NIEER) policy brief "The Targeted vs. Universal Debate: Should the United States Have Preschool for All?" sets forth clear evidence that middle-income children need to improve their school readiness through quality preschool education (Barnett, Brown, and Shore).

The Call for Universal Preschool

Since 2001, the American Federation of Teachers has been calling for universal preschool education (Wilgoren). Parents were calling for publicly funded pre-kindergarten programs even earlier ("Preschool for Everyone" 98). Business leaders as well have argued that "free, high quality preschool education for all children ages three and over" is crucial to the economic and social future of the United States ("Preschool for All" 8).

In 2004, after the release of their policy brief, the NIEER added its voice to the chorus of experts and families arguing for a nationwide system of quality preschools (Cardman). NIEER noted that "public support for preschool education is growing across the country," and that most states now offer funding for preschool programs. America seems determined to catch up to European countries such as France, where universal preschool education from age three has produced students who are "high achievers" in school, regardless of socio-economic background (Ferrandino and Tirozzi).

An Opportunity for Teachers and Library Media Specialists

The majority of parents in America already have their children in some kind of day care or preschool classroom (Barnett, Brown, and Shore). The National Institute for Early Education Research has argued that this is an opportunity for America to invest in proper resources for these children. As more early childhood education centers are developed, and education is extended from kindergarten to pre-kindergarten and preschool levels, educators will have to define what constitutes a quality preschool experience. As demand for properly trained and accredited early childhood educators grows, classroom teachers and library media specialists need to orient themselves to a younger population than they may have dealt with previously.

Children can learn much more in the early childhood years than we ever thought possible. The National Research Council's Committee on Early Childhood Pedagogy has stated that "young children are more capable learners than current practices reflect" (Bowman, Donovan, and Burns 2). If we are to address the special learning needs of the youngest students in our schools, teachers and library media specialists must expand their professional resources to include the growing population of preschool children in our schools.

Early Learning Standards

Concerns Over Standards

Not all states have standards for early childhood education, and those that do have only recently developed them (most since 2000). A lot of what is out there for the early years has been described as poorly written, vague, and inappropriate (Kendall 66). Early childhood educators warn of the dangers in watering down standards for older students to create guidelines for teaching our very youngest children (Kendall 65).

The International Reading Association and the National Association for the Education of Young Children have published a joint position paper on this issue, claiming that all too often early literacy educators use "inappropriate teaching practices suited to older children or adults perhaps but ineffective with children in preschool, kindergarten, and the early grades" (2). Too many programs for children focus exclusively on cognitive development, creating a program that is too academic for the early years of schooling.

Despite these concerns, early learning standards are becoming increasingly common. Scott-Little, Kagan, and Frelow, in their important study of state-level standards (*Creating the Conditions for Success with Early Learning Standards: Results from a National Study of State-Level Standards for Children's Learning Prior to Kindergarten*), note that "pressure has been mounting to develop early learning standards." The challenge for early childhood educators is to ensure that the unique characteristics of young children are acknowledged in the writing and application of such standards.

The Pre-K Difference

There is a Pre-K difference! First of all, it is normal to find a much wider variation in skills and ability to perform tasks in the preschool years. Children grow and develop quickly, but at varying rates. This accounts for what Kagan and Scott-Little describe as "a deep-seated and long-standing skepticism toward learning standards among the early childhood community." (388) Differences between children in these early years can be extreme. Educators fear that assessments linked to high-stakes standards could result in some young children being judged as unready or ill-equipped for promotion to a new grade or program.

The strict application of grade-level benchmarks has been rejected by the National Association for the Education of Young Children (NAEYC) and the National Association of Early Childhood Specialists in State Departments of Education (NAECS/SDE) in a joint statement entitled *Early Learning Standards: Creating the Conditions for Success*. Effective early learning standards should be "flexible descriptions . . . of developmental continua" that may "refer" to a certain age group, but that should not be "tightly linked" to the evaluation of all children of that age (5). They go on to encourage teachers to "create adaptations" to standards that will "promote success for all children" (5).

The Need to Address the Individual Child

Thus, learning standards must be set for the individual child, not the grade level. Educators need to challenge children to perform to the best of their ability, without making demands that cannot be achieved. This is why formative assessment is so important for children in this age range. It allows teachers to learn – through close observation of learning processes – just where children are in their development of skills, knowledge, and positive dispositions, and what they need to further this development.

How Standards Address the Individual Child

Fortunately there are signs that the recommendations of NAEYC and NAECS/SDE are being taken into account by states developing early learning standards. In the preamble to Georgia's content standards for pre-kindergarten, the need to adapt standards to each individual child is clearly stated: "Because Pre-K children learn and develop at varying rates, instruction must be planned to meet each child's individual needs" (Georgia Department of Early Care and Learning). Scott-Little, Kagan, and Frelow note in their survey that "states have been highly cognizant of the potential for negative consequences for individual children as they have developed standards".

Social and Emotional Factors

Social and emotional factors are intrinsic to the learning processes of very young children. If children cannot relate the class curriculum to their own lives, there is little likelihood that they will be motivated to participate in inquiry activities. The need for meaningful curriculum content (over arbitrarily assigned topics) is referred to as "authentic curriculum," "integrated curriculum," or "informal learning." The child should be able to relate content to their previous experiences.

Authentic curriculum can occur spontaneously, such as when children ask questions or raise issues that have not been planned by the teacher. Such instances should be taken advantage of whenever they occur. However, as a teacher's knowledge of her students and of the typical traits of a particular age group grows, content can be selected that is very likely to be greeted with enthusiasm by young learners. In fact, all projects that are planned with authenticity in mind should then have to pass the test of student interest and motivation before they are pursued for days, weeks, or months of the school year. Children can be primed for a new project idea, of course, by having them participate in hands-on experiences that widen their personal knowledge of the world and stimulate new interest in topics as they grow in firsthand experience.

How Standards Address Social and Emotional Factors

Again, signs are good that states are taking social and emotional needs into account as they develop early learning standards. Scott-Little, Kagan, and Frelow examined 29 early learning standards from 27 states and found that 19 of these documents addressed the social-emotional developmental domain.

Physical and Nutritional Needs

As well as needing to relate to curriculum content, children need to feel secure if they are to learn. Their physical and nutritional needs have to be taken into consideration. This is why the old debate in early education circles between centers that *care* for children and preschools that *educate* children has been abandoned. Educators today realize that quality early childhood education necessarily involves *both* care and education. Physical needs go beyond just safety concerns. Children have an innate desire for movement, physical activity, and free play that cannot be ignored.

How Standards Address Physical and Nutritional Needs

Scott-Little, Kagan, and Frelow analyzed state early learning standards for the developmental domain of physical health. Of the 27 states surveyed, 20 had included this domain in their standards documents.

The Importance of Non-Academic Strengths

A strictly academic approach, which addresses only their cognitive development, is sure to fail because it neglects these other essential components of how learning takes place for young children. In fact, academically geared programs for young children may even destroy innate positive dispositions such as curiosity and eagerness to learn (Katz and Chard 36). Besides, recent research has found that "nonacademic strengths such as emotional competence or positive 'approaches to learning' when children enter kindergarten are strong predictors of academic skills in later grades" (NAEYC and NAECS/SDE). These positive approaches to learning – also known as "desirable dispositions" – are high on the list of outcomes that teachers most want to see in their students, yet, as Katz and Chard point out, they are "rarely . . . considered worthy of being evaluated in early childhood education" (36).

Dispositions have been defined as "temperament" or "personality traits" (Driscoll and Nagel 35; Katz and Chard 34). But this does not mean that they are not amenable to change and development. As we shall see, the project approach to teaching helps young children develop many positive habits of mind and behavior: persistence in the face of a difficult problem, curiosity about new concepts, motivation to learn, cooperativeness, and even humor. Dispositions include many intellectual traits such as the simple desire to make sense of our experiences and to make predictions about observed phenomena.

Early childhood education should include a conscious effort on the part of teachers to create learning environments and activities that allow children to practice and experience these desirable behaviors. Katz and Chard insist that this is an important part of the work of an early childhood educator: "Identifying and observing children's dispositional development should thus be taken into account in teacher decision making" (38). This is why the activities in the following chapters make explicit mention of intellectual and social dispositions.

How Standards Address Non-Academic Strengths

Turning again to the survey of early learning standards by Scott-Little, Kagan, and Frelow, the inclusion of dispositions or attitudes toward learning is less prevalent than other developmental domains. "Approaches to learning" is defined in their March 2005 research report, *Inside the Content: The Breadth and Depth of Early Learning Standards*, as including four indicators: curiosity; initiative; reflection and interpretation; and invention and imagination. This dimension of early childhood learning was addressed in only seven of the standards documents. However, in standards that do address this issue, additional dispositions are listed. Arizona's Social Emotional Standard covers dispositions in "Strand 4: Approaches to Learning." They include six essential dispositions: curiosity, initiative, persistence, creativity, problem-solving, and confidence. More social and intellectual dispositions are provided in *Figure 1.1*, *Dispositions*, at the end of this chapter.

The Project Approach to Learning

A Child-Centered Approach

The project approach to learning is designed with the distinctive characteristics of early childhood in mind. This child-centered approach allows individuals to work at their level of skill, comfort, and interest. Children are given choices throughout the life of a project in terms of what questions they want to ask and what kinds of work they would like to produce as part of their investigation. The teacher acts as a facilitator, providing materials and hands-on experiences for the children, supporting their discussions and problem solving, and ensuring that motivation remains high throughout the life of the project. Thus, the critical components of early childhood education that were noted earlier (allowing for wide differences in level of development, acknowledging social and emotional needs, and designing learning activities that are challenging yet achievable by all) are admirably addressed by this approach to learning.

Researchers and practitioners agree that young children are natural and keen explorers of their environments, with an "innate desire to learn" (NAEYC and NAECS/SDE). Because children need a great deal of assistance to develop their understandings, the role of the adult is "crucial" to learning (Mallett 1). Thus concepts such as Bruner's idea of scaffolding, Vygotsky's zone of proximal development, and Piaget's notion of adaptation are crucial to the project approach.

Characteristics of the Project Approach

The project approach allows children to explore a theme or topic in depth. Diffily and Sassman (6) list the following as the essential characteristics of a project:

- student directed
- connected to the real world
- research based
- informed by multiple resources
- embedded with knowledge and skills
- conducted over time
- concluded with an end product.

Lasting anywhere from a few days, to weeks, or even months, the process is defined in three stages: beginning the project (Phase I), developing the project (Phase II), and concluding the project (Phase III) (Helm and Katz 9).

A project kicks off with discussions of topics that are relevant to the children. As they share their knowledge and prior experiences, the teacher collects and helps to organize their questions. Next a series of investigations takes place, including field trips, guest speakers with expert knowledge, examination of real objects or artifacts, reading and being read to, studying pictures, and role playing (Driscoll and Nagel 159). Because it is so democratic in nature, the project approach can lead up many blind alleys. Sometimes children come up with ideas that would be difficult or impossible to realize. When this happens, the adults may have to gently guide the children to a route that is more likely to lead them to success. As Diffily and Sassman note, sometimes the "wonderings" of their adult facilitator may have to be quite directive if the project is not to derail (17). When to use such spoken musings about how to fix a problem is always a judgment call on the part of the teacher or librarian currently working with the students.

Projects generally achieve closure through a presentation where children share what they have learned with other children, parents, or classmates. This final presentation is decided upon by the children at the beginning or middle stage of the project. This model might be something that the children have seen during a field trip, that an expert demonstrates, or that the teacher collects or constructs herself. The important thing is that the children have a model to follow. A list, *Potential End Products*, is provided in *Figure 1.2* at the end of this chapter.

Curriculum Connections

The project approach is not all that is happening in a good early childhood classroom. Regular instruction takes place as well. But this does not mean that there is a huge gulf between regular lessons and a current project. In fact, projects can and should feed into the skills and knowledge covered by the school's official curriculum. A class that is exploring a topic through the project approach can make use of the materials and discoveries of the project so far in lessons about math concepts, language learning, science, art, technology, or music.

Integrating Standards into the Project Approach

The project approach to learning does not preclude the integration of early learning standards or content-area standards. Curriculum goals can easily be achieved during a project or with project materials. For example, preschool children who have been examining hats in a project can learn to count them and sort them. Likewise, investigations during the project and work on the final product may call for a lesson in how to measure with a ruler, how to draw a comparative chart, how to write a list, or how to assign roles. These tasks require new skills that are most likely part of the linguistic, conceptual, and social competencies that the curriculum is written to achieve.

Early learning standards can be achieved while doing a project. In chapters three through seven, the first project description includes a sampling of early learning standards that could be easily integrated into the classroom and library activities. These standards are derived from the five "indicators used to code standards" used by Scott-Little, Kagan, and Frelow (3), the Pre-K to Grade Two standards developed by the National Council for the Teaching of Mathematics, and early learning and content-area standards from the states of Arizona, California, Georgia, and Illinois.

Collaboration

A crucial role of the library media specialist in promoting collaborative efforts will be to convince teachers that their content standards and indicators are a natural fit with the project approach. For this reason, an early planning sheet for a project should clearly define not only the role of the teacher and librarian, but also note the early learning and content-area standards that will be integrated into the project activities. *Figure 1.3, Collaborative Planning Sheet*, at the end of this chapter makes this link to standards clear. Of course, projects are fluid and flexible. As questions arise there may be new opportunities to integrate standards. These should be noted on the back of the sheet for future reference if the project is repeated.

The essential feature of the project approach is that everyone is active and motivated to learn. In this context of highly motivated and relevant learning, children can profitably experience their first investigation of informational resources. The following chapters provide examples of projects that will work with children from preschool through grade two. These projects are described as they might unfold from the questioning and planning of phase one through to the end product. Clearly, the course of a project cannot be predicted the moment that an interesting topic for investigation is conceived. No crystal ball can predict how children's minds will direct the project. That said, the teacher and librarian could help to stimulate interest in projects that are doable with resources at hand.

Resources

The question of resources is sometimes a sticking point with teachers. Some teachers complain that it is difficult to collect enough resources that will sufficiently answer questions and still be accessible to young children. The librarian has a critical role to play in addressing these concerns. Once teachers and librarians agree on a list of typical project ideas that will have real appeal to young children, it is time to start collecting appropriate resources. This does not have to cost the moon. Materials with clear photographs and images can be used with preschool students, while the written material might make the book appropriate to use again in grade ones or two.

With projects, as with real life, we do not learn everything there is to know about a subject in a single research project. When preschool children investigate a topic, their questions and understandings are those of a three-year-old child. A kindergarten or grade one class that takes up the same topic will use the same resources differently and will develop an end product that reflects their more advanced thinking. Resources are often appropriate to a range of ages, thus it makes sense to revisit topics as children develop in skills and knowledge. Several of the projects in this book will be explored at two different grade levels to give teachers and librarians a sense of how this is possible.

Social Dispositions

- ☑ Listening to others speak
- ☑ Waiting your turn to speak
- ☑ Working as a team
- ☑ Helping others who are having difficulty
- ☑ Recognizing each person's unique contribution
- ☑ Appreciating the work of others
- ☑ Recognizing that people have different strengths and weaknesses
- ☑ Empathizing with others
- ☑ Showing concern when others are upset or having difficulty
- ☑ Asking permission from others
- ☑ Sharing

Intellectual Dispositions

- ☑ Curiosity
- ☑ Desire to find answers
- ☑ Perseverance when faced with a challenging problem
- ☑ Creativity
- ☑ Initiative
- ☑ Desire to make predictions and check predictions
- ☑ Desire to synthesize information
- ☑ Desire to be accurate

Figure 1.2: Potential End Products

Potential End Products

Potential End Product	Description of End Product	Potential Audience
Book	A bound volume of children's work	Parents
Bulletin Board Display	Drawing and artistic expressions	Visitors
Calendar	Month or school year with thematic design	Students
Celebration	Theme party, special day, school announcements	Students
Construction	Usually large and interactive, built by students	Students
Demonstration	How to do something (live or filmed)	Students
Discovery Center	Interactive experiments	Students
Documentary	Each stage of project is recorded	Parents
Dramatic Play	Informal scenarios acted by students	Teacher
Environmental Project	Change to the grounds of the school	Community
Fair	Children work at a variety of kiosks	Community
Interview	Conversation with an expert (filmed)	Students
Letter	Written with the goal of effecting change	Any
List	Enumerated information or procedure	Students
Model	A small-scale reproduction	Parents
Mockup	A reproduction of a milieu for dramatic play	Students
Museum	Cultural or natural artifacts	Any
News Report	Informational broadcast (filmed)	Any
Parade	Involving costumes, props, music or song	Community
Picture or Photo Gallery	Evidence organized for viewing	Any
Poster	Information presented with words and pictures	Any
Presentation	Objects and information explained	Students
Role Plays	Small groups take on roles related to project	Students
Thematic Door	Graphic information presented on classroom door	Visitors
Thematic Mascot	A human figure is created and dressed by theme	Students
Puppet Show	Information is presented via puppets	Students
Video Presentation	More complex oral presentations are recorded	Parents

Collaborative Planning for Project-Based Learning

Project is relevant? _____

CLASSROOM   Discussion   LIBRARY
                                                         MEDIA CENTER

Investigation

End Product

Early Learning Standards to be integrated

Chapter Two

Putting Research Into Practice

Informational Resources in the Early Years

Most children come to preschool with some experience of informational resources. Early "toy" books such as pop-up books or "lift the flap" books, concept books and alphabet books, narrative and non-narrative nonfiction, and even storybooks contain real information of interest to young children, to say nothing of information beamed at them from televisions and computers. Mallett notes that at first very young children (aged six to 15 months) simply treat books as toys. Even children as young as nine months will take an interest in books that include interesting textures, sounds, or movements. As they head towards two years of age, they begin to respond to pictures in books and even match objects represented in books to their real-life equivalents by pointing to or naming these objects (Mallett 28).

Researchers tell us that young children learn best hands-on. In fact, children arrive at preschool having spent most of their lives engaging their five senses in a firsthand exploration of everything around them. Young parents know just how difficult it is to keep toddlers from touching hot stoves, grabbing the family cat, and putting any small object they encounter directly into their mouths. Seeing, touching, smelling, tasting, and listening continue to be of primary importance to learning throughout the early childhood years, yet forays can be made into less direct sources of information.

Advantages of the Project Approach

The educating of children can be approached in two ways: the traditional instructional approach in which the teacher is the expert teaching the children a new skill or concept and the project approach in which the children are given the power to choose what they will study and how they will go about it. While there is a place for both approaches in the education of young children, the project approach is best suited to a child's first use of informational texts, for several reasons.

First of all, the explorations undertaken in the project approach come from the child's own world. Thus, the topics are directly relevant to the child. This leads to the second advantage of the project approach: The children are motivated to learn because the topic is meaningful to them. This motivation should be sustained throughout the project as the children raise questions and plan activities and outcomes. And as questions are raised, the desire for information sources grows. This information can come from experts, observations during field trips, or informational texts. Thirdly, we know that children learn best by exploring their world directly. The project approach places emphasis on first-hand experience before secondary sources of information are introduced. This in turn relates to the final advantage: the need for background knowledge. Children will make more sense of secondary information if they already have experience of a subject through discussion with peers and adults, questioning, and a workable vocabulary (both visual and oral). Because the project approach looks at a topic in depth, children are able to build a substantial knowledge base before they tackle information in the form of pictures and text. The beauty of the project approach is that it gives *all* the children common, first-hand experience that they can recognize when they go to secondary sources of information.

The project approach allows children to use all the skills and dispositions that they will need to tackle any problem or question throughout their lives. Children taking part in a project are encouraged to:

- ask questions
- seek out information
- interpret information (visual and textual) that they see, hear, or read
- record their findings with the help of the teacher or library media specialist
- plan, debate, discuss, and make decisions
- represent their new understandings through drawings, charts, models, video, or text
- work on informational displays and constructions
- share their knowledge with others
- cooperate to achieve a common goal
- recognize that everyone brings his or her own particular skills to a project
- display all of the important intellectual and social dispositions required to solve real world problems.

Using Informational Resources

Many teachers of young children are reluctant to use informational texts. Often teachers believe that stories are more appropriate for young students. Some teachers consider informational texts too difficult or too boring for children. Another obstacle might be a lack of training in how to integrate nonfiction into an early childhood program. However, research has proven that children enjoy and desire informational texts. Given the choice, children will pick "informational books, magazines, and other materials" (Walker, Kragler, Martin, and Arnett). As Linda Hoyt points out in her book *Make It Real: Strategies for Success with Informational Texts*, children need exposure to nonfiction if they are to be expected to broach nonfiction books and textbooks as they progress through the upper levels of elementary school.

> Reading fiction will not necessarily help you be better at reading a cookbook, directions, or a computer manual. To become successful readers and writers of informational texts, children must see, hear, and write informational texts from the onset of literacy development. (39)

And if they are introduced within the wider context of an in-depth project, even young school children can derive pleasure and meaning from nonfiction.

Kinds of Informational Books

Nonfiction Picture Books

Several kinds of informational texts can be used with young children. Chapter 3 includes a book called *Which Hat Is That?* While it features a young mouse dressed in human clothes and trying on hats, it is essentially a nonfiction book about identifying different kinds of hats. That the information is expressed in creative language ("When I wear a tall white puffy hat, a spiffy hat, a spotless hat . . .") does not make it any less an informational text. That it is also a book that features talking animals (what is referred to as "ourselves in furs" by writers on children's literature) does not detract from its excellent informational value. This book is likely to be cataloged in the fiction section of the school library as a picture book, but it is patently not a storybook. We can call this kind of book a nonfiction picture book. A very similar book, *Whose Nose Is This?* by Wayne Lynch, is cataloged as nonfiction because it uses photographs of real animals and contains more "real" information in the text.

Informative Stories

Many of the stories that teachers and library media specialists already use with children convey information about the real world. Though these are narratives, they can also be informative. Take for example *Dog's Colorful Day* by Emma Dodd. As the subtitle indicates, this is a story with information: *A Messy Story about Colors and Counting*. The narrative follows Dog through his perambulations around the yard and the city, where the black spot on his ear is joined by other spots – ice cream, mud, orange juice, and other colorful accidents.

At the end of the story the author reviews the spots, having the children name the colors and count the spots, thus making its informational use explicit. A similar story would be Leo Lionni's *Little Blue and Little Yellow* or a similar, but more recently published book, *The Big Blue Spot* by Peter Holwitz. These are narrative in structure, but the stories are also informative lessons about mixing paints to get a new color. We can call these books informative stories. These and many other books from the picture book fiction section can make read-alouds in the early stages of a project, before true nonfiction works are introduced.

Narrative Nonfiction

A third kind of information text is what Margaret Mallet calls "narrative non-fiction" (91). These are true works of nonfiction, but they follow a story format or step-by-step procedure that has the feel of a story. An example would be *From Seed to Sunflower* by Gerald Legg, which uses illustrations to explain the lifecycle of a sunflower. A similar book using photographs is *Life Cycle of a Sunflower* by Angela Royston. Even a wordless book like *Truck* by Donald Crews or *Alphabet City* by Stephen T. Johnson has information about the real world to impart and the logical sequence of a narrative.

True Nonfiction

The final type of informational book is true nonfiction. This kind of book does not have a narrative structure. Allan Fowler's *What's the Weather Today?* from the "Rookie Read-About Science" series is a good example. While its text is simple and spare, it tackles the fairly complex topic of weather and climate and even includes an index. More advanced informational texts such as *Why Should I Brush My Teeth? And Other Questions about Healthy Teeth* by Louise Spilsbury include the sorts of informational graphics and layout of adult books: charts, boxes, differently sized headings, paragraphs that snake around photos, sidebars, and captioned photographs. Though it is only 32 pages long, it is divided into short chapters and includes an index and bibliographical references.

Approaches to Information Sources

Children's approaches to informational sources will vary depending on age and ability. Whether they are working with classmates or listening to a read-aloud, very young children will be "reading" the visual information in the text. Emergent readers will start to notice and comment on print, especially as they learn to identify letters. Even children who are capable of reading will depend on visual information to help them interpret the text. When responding to nonfiction, young children can use drawings, constructions, or scribed text to represent their understanding of a topic. As we will see in the following chapters, there are many ways to help engage children with informational books.

Dialogic Reading

A child's repertoire of reactions and ways of trying to connect to a text are infinitely varied and spontaneous. Yet teachers and librarians can and should encourage this engaged response through an animated and aware dialogic reading. This approach encourages interruptions to the text as children respond. It allows for commenting, clapping, movement, laughing, and questioning to bring elements of the stories to life. The National Research Council explains dialogic reading in this way:

> Dialogic reading involves several changes in the way adults typically read books to children. Central to these changes is a shift in roles. During typical shared reading, the adult reads and the child listens, but in dialogic reading the child learns to become the storyteller. The adult assumes the role of an active listener, asking questions, adding information, and prompting the child to increase the sophistication of descriptions of the material in the picture book. (196)

Grover J. Whitehurst, who helped develop this method of reading to children at the Stony Brook Reading and Language Project, explains it like this:

> In dialogic reading, the adult helps the child become the teller of the story. The adult becomes the listener, the questioner, and the audience for the child. No one can learn to play the piano just be listening to someone else play. Likewise, no one can learn to read just by listening to someone else read. Children learn most from books when they are actively involved.

This is true of not just storybooks but informational texts as well.

Peer Sequences

Dialogic reading proceeds by means of short exchanges between the adult reader and the child. These exchanges are called PEER sequences, which stands for *Prompts*, *Evaluates*, *Expands*, and *Repeats* (Whitehurst). The adult asks children something about the text she has just read or about the pictures that accompany the text. This is the *prompt*. When the child responds, the adult *evaluates* the response and then *expands* upon it, thus giving the children more information about the text and modeling how adults make sense of what they read. Finally, the adult will repeat the original prompt to make sure that the child understands what has just been expanded upon.

Not all PEER sequences are made up of questions. A simple comment such as "I see many interesting animals in Nora's bedroom" can elicit comments from the children who are listening to a dialogic reading. The National Research Council suggests when this approach is used with two- and three-year-olds, the questioning should be limited to the page in the book that is currently being read. By the time children reach four and five years of age, the sequence can involve commentary on the story or content of the whole book, or connections between elements in the narrative and the child's own life. Most importantly, they underscore the fact that dialogic reading is simply a conversation between an adult and children. It should not interfere with the enjoyment of the story or text.

Dialogic Reading of Stories

When reading a story, dialogic reading can help the adult to evaluate the children's understanding of what is going on. For example, in *A Hat for Minerva Louise*, the adult reader might ask (the prompt) "Who is Minerva talking to?" The children would identify the scarecrow in the story. "That's right," the adult would say (the evaluation). "Do you think that the scarecrow can hear her?" This expansion would draw attention to the fact that Minerva often misinterprets what she sees. Finally, the adult would repeat "No, the scarecrow can't hear her because he is just made of sticks and old clothes." If the children are very young, the expansion and repetition might be even simpler, such as asking the children if they can repeat the word "scarecrow." Later in the story, when Minerva believes that she has found a hat, the adult might ask "Can you see a hat in the picture?" Then the children might predict which object Minerva *thinks* is a hat. By the end of the story the children will probably have a lot to say about this silly little chicken.

Dialogic Reading of Nonfiction

Nonfiction texts are often first given to children when they are already readers. Adults assume that because children can read, they can also interpret a text fully on their own. Thus they are left to read them on their own, silently. Dialogic reading can help children learn how to approach informational books by hearing an adult think out loud as they gather information from the text, images, captions, and other cues typical of nonfiction. For example, when reading the simple informational book *Feeling Things* by Allan Fowler, the adult might ask "What has just happened to the girl in this photo?", thus giving the children a chance to interpret the image before the text – "Ouch! You stub your toe and it hurts!" – is read.

With a more complex information book such as *The Five Senses* by Sally Hewitt, the adult who is reading about touch might say, "I'm looking at the table of contents to see if this book about the senses has some information about touch. Can you see the word touch? What page is it on?" Once all the children have had a chance to find the word and the page number, the reader can sum up by saying "That's right. Everyone has found that the chapter on touch is on page 16." Once the reader turns to this page, the children can be led to explain what is happening in the pictures before the reader reads each section. Children can discover that reading an informational text is different from a story. After reading the "Try It Out!" box, the class might decide to test out the idea of putting objects into a pillowcase for their friends to guess at. Thus they will learn that books can give us information and ideas about topics that we choose. The children will see that nonfiction is not read in the same way as a storybook.

Prompts Using "CROWD"

A second mnemonic, CROWD, is used by Whitehurst to explain the five kinds of prompts that can be used. *Completion prompts* are those that ask the children to finish your sentence. This is especially appealing to kids when the text rhymes. *Recall prompts* ask the children to recall what happened in a book after it is read, or before it is read if the book is already familiar to the children. *Open-ended prompts* invite the children to describe what they see in a picture or photograph. *Wh- prompts* are the typical questions we ask – what, where, when, why, and how. Finally, *distancing prompts* ask the children to relate what they have discovered from a book to their own experience. This is especially useful in the course of a project because the children will have had many and varied shared experiences to talk about.

Completion prompts, open-ended prompts, and wh- prompts can be used with children from the age of three right through to grade two. Recall and distancing prompts are more difficult however, and will not work with children as young as three years of age (Whitehurst). Prompts help to engage the children with the text. No magic formula exists for what prompts and how many should be used with a story or information book. Prompts will be determined by the age and interests of the children. The adult reader needs to be sensitive to the way that the children are responding, and judge what kind of prompts to use based on that. Using dialogic reading should not make reading a chore. Passages can still simply be read aloud. Not everything needs to be commented upon. As Whitehurst notes, the most important thing to remember in a dialogic reading is – *"Keep it fun!"*

Print vs. Digital Sources of Information

e-Books

This book will focus on print sources of information. As more and more stories and nonfiction in print become available in e-book format, librarians may choose to collect both formats in nonfiction. Because e-books can be projected as large images, they are the ultimate "big book" for sharing with the whole class or large groups. The size and interactivity offers many advantages when employing informational strategies in the library and classroom.

Online Information

Subscription Databases

For projects at the lower elementary school level, students can begin to apply the search skills that they have practiced with books to online sources. In this case, the best choice is an online product designed specifically with young children in mind. One excellent product is the database for children *Kids InfoBits* from Thomson Gale. It has a graphic interface that is easy for lower elementary school students to interpret and use. In addition it gives a green dot or red triangle to all articles to indicate reading level. EBSCO's interface called *Kids Search* follows the same principle for its elementary database *Primary Search*, though its content is often too difficult for young readers to decipher on their own. Both offer plenty of photographs and diagrams that make excellent informational learning tools.

Internet

With the project approach one can never predict all the questions that children will ask. Children may ask questions during a project that no book, database, or available expert can answer. In this case, a mediated search on the Internet by an adult facilitator might be able to provide the answer so that the child can happily continue with the main work of the project.

Technology

The National Association for the Education of Young Children has published a position statement on this subject entitled Technology and Young Children – Ages 3 Through 8. NAEYC acknowledges that technology can have a "positive effect" on children's learning, but adds that "computers supplement and do not replace highly valued early childhood activities and materials, such as art, blocks, sand, water, books, exploration with writing materials, and dramatic play." (1) Educators have a responsibility to choose software and multimedia that are appropriate for children, especially since, according to the NAEYC, many titles in this area are of limited value (1).

Assessment

Marilou Hyson, in an article from *Educational Leadership* entitled "Putting Early Academics in Their Place," puts it simply: "Young children don't test well." Good teachers in early childhood education rely on a wide variety of assessment strategies. Rather than test children, teachers need to make formative evaluation a part of activities, through close observation, questioning, and discussion. Katz and Chard define the environment where this sort of assessment can take place as one of "optimal informality" (48). This requires a delicate balance of rules on the one hand (to prevent chaos from ensuing) and openness on the other (to allow children to feel free to express themselves). As they point out, this will only work if children are also taught ways in which they can alert their teacher when they are confused or have a question.

The NAEYC's position statement on developmentally appropriate practice advises that assessment of young children rely "heavily on the results of observations of children's development, descriptive data, collections of representative work by children, and demonstrated performance during authentic, not contrived, activities" (21). The project approach provides many opportunities to engage in all these forms of assessment.

Chapter Three

Research and Inquiry in Preschool

Working With Children in Preschool

Three-year-olds come to us from a wide variety of backgrounds. Some may have been in a day care as a toddler while others might have been at home with a parent or caregiver for the first three years. Thus their reactions during the first few weeks of school might range from tearful pleas for Mom to contented play and exploration of a new environment. Children will come from many cultural backgrounds, with different experiences of food, families, religion, dress, and language. Children might have had stories read to them by a parent every day, while others might never or rarely have shared a book with an adult. Some children might have very patient parents and relatives who listen to them and answer all their questions, other children may not be so lucky. However, once they are in preschool, they will have an opportunity to share many experiences, which will help each child develop and learn at her own pace.

Despite individual differences between children, there are broad principles to take into consideration when creating an appropriate classroom setting – both in the regular classroom and the library media center – for three-year-olds. These children need:

- a learning environment that emphasizes language, activity, and large muscle movement
- ample opportunity for dramatic play
- access to blocks, clay, and materials for drawing and scribbling
- to talk and share with the teacher and their peers

- to tell their own stories (as far as they are able at this age)
- to listen to stories.

Children's questions and opinions need to be taken seriously by the teacher or library media specialist because they are an important clue to not only their current thinking but to their interests as well. According to the NAEYC, curriculum at this age should be responsive to "the children's interests and ideas" (Bredekamp and Copple 131). The NAEYC sees these interests as an opportunity for learning: "Adults know that 3-year-olds' interest in babies, and especially their own recent infancy, is an opportunity for children to learn about themselves and human development" (Bredekamp 47).

Three-year-olds may sometimes revert to behavior that we would associate more with toddlers, and they can sometimes surprise us with statements and actions more typical of a four-year-old (Bredekamp and Copple 98). However, general statements of abilities and development can be made for this age group. We know that for the vast majority of children this age, their art will not look representational, though they will begin to design objects such as houses or people (Bredekamp and Copple 105). At this stage in their development their drawing and painting is limited to vertical, horizontal, and circular markings (Malley). Their participation in drawing and painting is more an outlet for self-expression than an exercise in representation. However, if children at this age are asked to draw something that they have seen, they will name the "objects" that they have drawn.

Children at this age may choose to watch other children playing, to engage in parallel play (playing alongside someone but not with them), or to take part in associative play (playing with the same toys and chatting, while still pursuing their own scenarios) (Bredekamp and Copple 117). Children need access to props related to curriculum activities so that they can explore their understandings of these new concepts when they feel the need. The presence of these props will also stimulate dramatic play related to newly acquired understandings and vocabulary. Adults who work with children should work to create opportunities for these forms of play to take place. The knowledge acquired during projects will encourage high-level dramatic play from children.

Children will have varying abilities to listen and sit still. Some children may have trouble sitting up for more than a few minutes. Some children may even wonder away from a reading to engage in private play. The NAEYC recommends that children be free to "enter or leave the group at will" (Bredekamp 48). However, if a reading and the songs, fingerplays, and movements that accompany it are interesting to the children, this should not be a problem most of the time. A crucial consideration is that the size of the group is not too large at this age.

Creating an Age-Appropriate Classroom

Having a designated area for listening to stories and informational books read aloud is important. It should be marked out as a specific spot and consistently used for read alouds and discussions. Make the idea of speaking in turns more concrete through an object such as a "talking ball." This ball can be rolled or passed from one child to another or to the teacher or librarian as each person speaks. The NAEYC tells us that allowing children to talk is very important at this stage (more so than listening skills). Children need to express themselves if their language is to improve. Teachers and librarians need to practice eliciting comments and questions from the children, rather than simply lecturing them.

Three-year-olds have already mastered many skills: "sitting, walking, toilet training, using a spoon, scribbling, and sufficient hand-eye coordination to catch and throw a ball" (Feiler and Tomonari 276). Yet they may still not have enough body/spatial awareness to avoid banging into things. Thus, the preschool classroom and library should be easy to navigate. Sharp edges on shelving units should be covered with soft plastic or rubber corner protectors. There should not be too much furniture to get in the way of a child's movements. Library media specialists who serve both preschool and elementary school students might clear one section of tables and chairs so that preschoolers could have an open area to sit for readings and activities.

At this stage children are still developing a sense of temporal awareness. These children may not react to bells and may not realize if you miss something from their regular routine. Their sense of independence is growing and they like to be able to do things for themselves. Students at this age should be given plenty of opportunities to try, with appropriate scaffolding from the teacher. Reminders about good behavior and rules are necessary. Three-year-olds are still learning how to share. Children should be provided with enough materials for exploration so that they do not have to compete over objects.

Preschool aged children have characteristic ways of thinking. For instance, they have a tendency to focus on "one piece of information when multiple pieces are relevant" (Driscoll and Nagel 51). This cognitive characteristic is known as centration.

Three-year-olds are still grappling with the difference between real and imaginary. The problem here is that they may not even ask you if they are unsure (Malley). A reading of *Go Away Big Green Monster*, a story which normally helps children conquer their fears as the parts of the monster's face are made to disappear, may be entertaining for most children in a group, but one child might take it for a real monster and burst into tears. Even puppets of spiders or witches might strike a child as frightening, so it is always important to emphasize the fact that they are not real and can't hurt us. Thankfully, these intense emotional reactions don't last long and children can be talked through them.

At this stage in their cognitive development, children have trouble remembering things. These children have yet to develop "memory strategies" (Driscoll and Nagel 51). Their powers of reasoning are present, but they feel free to invent an explanation for an event that they do not understand.

A knowledge of what can be expected (in general terms) from three-year-olds, coupled with firsthand experience talking, listening, and observing them, can help teachers and librarians in the selection of appropriate texts for use within a project. Generally, books that can be comprehended by these young children in a read-aloud tend to have a reading level of less than Grade Two level. Pictures are accompanied by a brief text. Rhyme, rhythm, and the repetition of words so common in children's books are important features to look for.

The most important of all is that the visual elements of the book are clear and comprehensible by three-year-olds. A book with simple text but dark, detailed, "busy" or complex pictures will not work at this level. One tricky picture book is *Hello, Red Fox* by Eric Carle. While it is a model of simplicity in text (reading level 2.2) and images, the idea of staring at one brightly colored picture to create a faint phantom afterimage of another picture in a different color is way beyond the cognitive capabilities of preschool children. Other books may have clear illustrations, but the conceptual content of the images may be difficult, as with many books by Chris Van Allsburg. Sometimes picture books with clear and engaging photos or illustrations may not work with the text that the author has written. Don't hesitate to use these books anyway, concentrating on a dialogic reading of the pictures, while largely ignoring the text.

Once selections are made, you are ready to share books through dialogic reading. Then the real fun begins. Children who gather to listen to a story or informational text enter into the experience of the narrative like no other audience. Children will ask questions, imitate sounds, move to the beat of the rhythms within the text, and recognize and comment on what they see in the pictures. It is common for children to point out letters that they recognize, especially the first letter of their own name. The story may stimulate them to relate certain elements to their own experience. Children are truly active participants in a reading and help to bring the text alive through their comments and actions. Their engagement with the text goes well beyond what even the most responsive older audience might exhibit during a public reading. Young people incorporate movement into their enjoyment of the text, using hands, feet, or even their whole body to respond. Their senses respond as they reach out to touch or point to elements in the story.

Some teachers and librarians think that "lessons" will destroy the fun of sitting back and listening to a good story. At first blush, this seems reasonable. After all, we all enjoy listening to a good story. However, for those who have firsthand experience of reading aloud to children, "just sitting back" is rarely the scenario one meets. Nor should it be. Children need to actively participate to make sense of stories – and informational texts as well. Teachers and library media specialists are there to help them get the most out of these experiences.

Informational Strategies in Preschool

Children in preschool are pre-readers. At this early stage of emergent literacy, fundamental cognitive concepts along with mental and physical skills are learned. Teachers and librarians can reinforce these understandings through dialogic readings, storytelling, dramatic play, sing-a-longs, repetition of sounds, and explicit comments while reading, writing, or drawing with the children. In this way, children grow in their awareness of print and sounds.

- Through questions about pictures in stories and nonfiction, children become aware of the fact that pictures in books represent objects in the real world.

- Through dialogic reading, children learn both to listen and to respond to information.

- Early "note-taking" by the teacher and librarian helps children see that pictures and words can represent ideas.

- Drawing and scribbling allows children to practice expressing themselves in "print."

- By labeling children's drawings according to the children's descriptions, children become aware of the use of words as labels.

- In the library and classroom, a rich print environment gives children opportunities to handle books properly and become familiar with particular books.

- Through practice turning pages of books, children learn that books are read from left to right.

- Pretending to read books to themselves, their peers, or puppets allows children to mimic real literacy.

- Stories are used to improve vocabulary and raise awareness of a subject before nonfiction sources are shared with children.

- By listening to stories and responding to nonfiction, children improve their attention span and learn how to regulate their physical activity.

- Through dramatic play, children practice new vocabulary and play with language and sounds.

- By having books re-read to them, children learn to recognize a book by the cover art.

- Because of the secure emotional bond that children share with their teacher and librarian, they are ready to engage in a shared experience of stories and nonfiction.

- Through dialogic readings of fiction and nonfiction, children learn that they can create meaning from text and images.

- Documenting investigations with digital photos and scribed captions allows children to represent their understandings just as books do.

- If a book has clear and interesting pictures, but advanced or wordy text, the teacher or librarian should allow a dialogic reading by the children of the pictures and ignore the text altogether.

Projects

PROJECT ONE: *Hats*

 ### Relevance

Preschool children are often required to bring a hat that can be left in the classroom. In warm weather months, a sun hat ensures that children always have protection from sunburn and UV rays when they are playing outside. Thus, as children begin their preschool year, hats are a relevant part of their lives. Later in the year, when weather turns colder, children may be required to have a winter hat at school to help keep their heads warm. Either way, children have a personal and concrete example of a hat with which to begin their investigation. Once the library media specialist has ensured that there are enough good stories and nonfiction books on this topic, it is time to complete a collaborative planning sheet with the preschool teacher.

 ### Discussion

The discussion can begin with an examination of their hats in class, with the teacher reinforcing and repeating words that they use to describe their hats. After the children have gathered their hats and sat in a semi-circle in the reading area, the discussion begins. The teacher can use a talking ball to ask children to comment in turn about their hats.

The children might talk about the color of their hats and whether the hats are soft or hard. Ask them to demonstrate which way the hats go on their heads. The teacher can help to increase their hat vocabulary by adding words like "brim" or "peak" to the discussion. ("Yes Susan, your hat is yellow and it has a wide brim around it." "Yes Matthew, your hat is a baseball cap and in front it has a peak. What is the peak for?") The teacher can take "notes" as the children discuss their hats by drawing each hat on white poster paper as each child describes his hat, marking the child's name under each one. This poster can then become part of the classroom display: "Our Hats." This discussion can conclude with questions about why we have to wear our hats when we go outside to play.

A fun way to start things off in the library is for the library media specialist to hide a frog puppet under her own hat, pulling it out after telling the following rhyme by David McCord: "I have a dog,/ I have a cat./ I've got a frog/ Inside my hat" (Robinson 9). The frog can then be used to help with questions and dialogic readings throughout this project. (Since frogs don't wear hats, the children have a lot to teach him).

Sarah Weeks has another good song about hats called "I Am Not a Hat," in which an egret argues that her feathers should not be made into a hat. Short poems, songs, and fingerplays are a good way to get a discussion with small children rolling. A picture book (from Sarah Weeks again) called *Who's Under That Hat* is a good opening read-aloud. This lift-the-flap book features common types of hats with various creatures under them, such as a Dalmatian under a red fireman's hat. It would also be a good book to use later in the project about colors.

 ## Investigation

Once the investigation stage has begun, the librarian can reinforce the classroom discussion with stories about hats. One good story is *While You Were Chasing a Hat* by Lilian Moore. The poetic text can be read aloud with questioning interspersed, or the book can be treated as a wordless story, with commentary drawn from the children as they tell the story. Rosanne Litzinger's simple paintings follow a little girl and her father as they chase her hat. The double-spread pictures open with the moment just after the hat has blown off her head. The hat fills the second page – a big orange sun hat with a wide brim and a white ribbon. Children can be asked to describe the hat and explain what has happened. (Each illustration, from the cover to the conclusion, has the girl's hair blowing in the wind). The children can then describe where the hat goes and how they chase it (by boat, over hills, past trees, by a church, below some crows) until she finally catches her hat. To conclude the story the librarian might ask the kids what they can do to prevent their hats from blowing off on a windy day. Having a hat that ties under the neck can aid this discussion. Other good stories about hats on windy days are *The Windy Day* by Halima Below, *Whose Hat Is It?* by Valeri Gorbachev, and *Who Took the Farmer's Hat?* by Joan M. Lexau.

An appropriate and useful story about hats as children begin their class discussions about their own hats is *Hats!* by Kevin Luthardt. This book realistically portrays the emotions of children who are teased about a hat. The children resolve their own troubles by complimenting the bully's hat. He soon changes his attitude. Children will have lots to say about this almost wordless story. Another simple book about hats is *Zoe's Hats: A Book of Colors* by Sharon Lane Holm, which presents clear pictures of Zoe and her various hats. More imaginative and quirky stories about hats are *Caps for Sale: A Tale of a Peddler, Some Monkeys, and Their Monkey Business* by Esphyr Slobodkina and the more modern update of this traditional tale *The Hatseller and the Monkeys: A West African Folktale*, with authentic designs from Mali. Edward Lear's classic poem, *The Quangle Wangle's Hat* has had an inviting update with Louise Voce's warm watercolor cartoons.

Another good story about hats for this age group is *A Hat for Minerva Louise* by Janet Morgan Stoeke. This story takes place on a snowy day, so it would be especially suitable for a project on winter hats. Minerva Louise, the sweet but naïve chicken, ventures outside of the barn. The cold starts to bother her, so she begins to look for warm clothes, finally deciding that what she needs is a hat. Kids will laugh at the things the chicken mistakes for hats (a flower pot, a boot). Ask the children if these are good hats, and they are sure to tell you what they really are. At one point

Minerva Louise walks right under a row of hats hanging on the wall, thinking "There must be a hat around here somewhere." Ask the children if they can see hats, since many will recognize a baseball cap and a sun hat from the classroom discussion. A good follow-up story about getting dressed for winter is *Under My Hood I Have a Hat* by Karla Kuskin. Eileen Spinelli's *Do You Have a Hat?* is an informational book that asks the children about hats – "Do YOU have a hat?/ Something fuzzy, warm, and red,/ to keep the snowflakes off your head?"

Now that the children have a heightened awareness of hats in their lives, they are ready to learn about other hats. Experts can visit the classroom with examples of hats that they use for specific purposes. For instance, a teacher in the school might drive a motorcycle. He could bring in his helmet so that students could ask questions about it and experience how hard it is, how it straps on your head, and how heavy it is. Many of the children probably wear helmets when riding tricycles or have older siblings who wear bike helmets. This would make a good comparison with the motorcycle helmet, as would helmets for batters in baseball or goalies in hockey. Other examples of useful hats would be gardening hats, hard hats, chef hats (or hair nets that the cafeteria staff would wear), firefighting hats, fancy hats, and fun hats (such as a hat with mouse ears or bug eyes). Colleagues, parents, and community members can contribute their knowledge as children question them about their hats.

Children can reinforce their learning about hats by imitating the actions of someone who is wearing the hat (hammering like a construction worker in a hard hat, pretending to use a hose to put out a fire if they are a firefighter). As children learn about different kinds of hats, play hats for children in light plastic or cloth can be added to the classroom items available for dramatic play. Children should be encouraged to play at the kinds of jobs and activities that their hat-wearing visitors have discussed with them. An informational story to allow the librarian to link with this class discussion is *Hats* by Jane Belk Moncure. The "word bird" in the book tries on hats for various occupations and gathers the tools that would be appropriate to each.

Fingerplays and rhymes related to these hats can be learned. For example, the fingerplay "My Hammer Song" can be learned after someone speaks to the children about working with a construction hat on: "Jenny works with one hammer, one hammer, one hammer. Jenny works with one hammer. Then she works with two" (Cole and Calmenson 30-31). Because of the danger of children moving their heads around too violently, teachers and librarians might want to only do four of these verses – two for the two hands hammering and two more for the feet hammering. When children are shown a gardening hat, they can learn the rhyme that will allow them to mimic appropriate gardening actions. To the tune of "Farmer in the Dell" children can sing: "The farmer sows his seeds,/ The farmer sows his seeds./ Hi Ho the dairy-o,/ The farmer sows his seeds." Or to the tune of "Here We Go Round the Mulberry Bush," "This is the way we plant our seeds,/ Plant our seeds, plant our seeds./ This is the way we plant our seeds,/ Early in the morning" (Music & Songs: Garden). Rhymes, songs, and fingerplays not only encourage children to use new vocabulary, it will help them in developing scenarios in the dramatic play center.

Now children are ready for an informative storybook. In their next library session they can explore the various kinds of hats in the flip-the-flap question and answer book, *Which Hat Is That?* by Anna Grossnickle Hines. A fun read-aloud with great descriptive words, asks children to identify a gardening hat, a cooking hat, a firefighter's hat, a fancy ("tea party") hat, and a fun ("favorite") hat. The charming illustrations by LeUyen Pham provide visual clues to match the clues in the text. Classroom visits by experts have already exposed the children to these hats and more, so they should have the vocabulary and knowledge to guess the answers before each flap is opened.

Finally, a true information book can be introduced as the project builds to a conclusion. A nonfiction book similar to *Which Hat is That?* is *What's on My Head?* by Margaret Miller. This large board book features close-up photographs of babies wearing everything from a beanbag frog or bow to a firefighter's hat or a rubber duck. *Hats, Hats, Hats* by Ann Morris, is an nonfiction book with a very simple text about the kinds of hats people wear. Though the photographs were obviously taken all over the globe, most of the hats pictured will already be familiar to the students from their previous work on this topic. The hats in this text are sometimes named (cowboy hats, sun hats) and sometimes categorized (play hats, hard hats, soft hats).

Now that the children have a wider experience of hats, this informational text could be followed up in the classroom with an examination of the hats that have been accumulating over the course of the project. The children can be asked if they can classify the hats they have into groups such as hard hats and soft hats. As the National Research Council notes, "When children know a great deal about something – so much so that we can say they have achieved a principled organization of it – they can deploy hierarchical classification structures" (Bowman, Donovan, & Burns 41). At this point, the children are sufficiently prepared to take part in this kind of advanced thinking skill because of all their previous experiences.

The teacher can conclude the project with an art activity to create fun hats. (One final story that would complement this culminating activity is *Zara's Hats* by Paul Meisel, about a young girl who takes over her father's business making hats). The children can use paints, markers, or crayons to color strips of paper that are long enough to fit around the child's head afterwards. After the art works are completed, the teacher can wrap the strips of paper around the child's head and tape the ends together. This makes a good activity to schedule before snack or lunch break, since the children can then share comments and observations among themselves as they eat. This "hat party" can be a satisfying and memorable conclusion to their investigation into hats.

▶ End Product

Children might decide that they want to share this simple end product with an audience. One option would be to visit another class for a brief "hat parade" or have the principal visit them during their party. Later they can be hung from the ceiling to be enjoyed, taken home to parents, or added to the child's portfolio. If the project takes place around Halloween, the parade might incorporate hats as part of their Halloween disguises. *Halloween Hats* by Elizabeth Winthrop is a good choice for expanding the possible choices of headwear.

 ## Integrating Standards

Along the way there have been many opportunities for authentic assessment of the children's work. Comments from the teacher during dialogic readings can confirm to the children that their responses have communicated good information. The teacher can observe the children as they narrate with movement what they have learned about hats from visiting experts. The children have provided evidence of expanded vocabulary as their discussions of hats evolve. Important social dispositions, such as taking an interest in what others say, were evidenced in their early exploration of their own hats. Intellectual dispositions, such as the desire to discover the purpose of objects, were prevalent in their questioning of experts. Products, such as the teacher's note-taking poster and the fun hats, are evidence of the expression and thinking of the children.

Assessing this project in terms of the indicators in California's "3 Years to Pre-K" document, *The Desired Results*, shows that all five areas of development are addressed. Under "Social-Emotional Development," indicator number five refers to engagement in "pretend play activities with peers." Indicators 13, 14, 15, and 18 under "Language and Cognitive Development" are covered: engaging in conversations about an idea; participation in songs, rhymes, and stories; trying out new vocabulary; and acting out songs. Math indicators 22 and 27, using size words and describing how items are the same or different, are dealt with during this project. Literacy development takes place when children pretend to read books (indicator 33) or engage in a discussion about books during dialogic readings (indicator 34). Finally, motor skills are used when children use rhythmic movement during songs and rhymes.

The NCTM standards relating to indicators, such as prediction, sorting, comparing, and number, are present. Approaches to learning are in evidence as children express curiosity about the objects that guest speakers bring to class. Social and emotional development is addressed as children take an interest in the hats of other children. Even health and safety standards are met since the children are learning about the dangers of UV rays and how to protect one's head when riding a bike, playing hockey, or working on a construction site.

Resources for "Hats"

Fiction:

Caps for Sale: A Tale of a Peddler, Some Monkeys, and Their Monkey Business by Esphyr Slobodkina (HarperCollins, 1985)

A Hat for Minerva Louise by Janet Morgan Stoeke (Puffin Books, 1994)

Hats! by Kevin Luthardt (Albert Whitman, 2004)

Hats by Jane Belk Moncure, illustrated by Chris McEwan (Child's World, 2003)

The Hatseller and the Monkeys: A West African Folktale by Baba Wagué Diakité (Scholastic, 1999)

The Quangle Wangle's Hat by Edward Lear, illustrated by Louise Voce (Candlewick Press, 2005)

Under My Hood I Have a Hat by Karla Kuskin, illustrated by Fumi Kosaka (Laura Geringer Books, 2003)

While You Were Chasing a Hat by Lilian Moore, illustrated by Rosanne Litzinger (HarperCollins, 2001)

Who Took the Farmer's Hat? by Joan M. Lexau, illustrated by Fritz Siebel (HarperCollins, 1988)

Who's Under that Hat? by Sarah Weeks (Red Wagon Books, 2005)

Whose Hat Is It? by Valeri Gorbachev (HarperCollins, 2004)

The Windy Day by Halima Below, illustrated by Jacqueline White (Lester Publishing, 1994)

Zara's Hats by Paul Meisel (Dutton Children's Books, 2003)

Information Books:

Do You Have a Hat? by Eileen Spinelli (Simon and Schuster Books for Young Readers, 2004)

Halloween Hats by Elizabeth Winthrop (Henry Holt, 2002)

Hats, Hats, Hats by Ann Morris, photographs by Ken Heyman (Mulberry Books, 1989)

What's on My Head? by Margaret Miller (Little Simon, 1998)

Which Hat Is That? by Anna Grossnickle Hines, illustrated by LeUyen Pham (Harcourt, 2002)

Zoe's Hats: A Book of Colors and Patterns by Sharon Lane Holm (Boyds Mills Press, 2003)

Other Fiction Books:

Aunt Flossie's Hats (And Crab Cakes Later) by Elizabeth Fitzgerald Howard, illustrated by James Ransome (Clarion, 2001)

Aunt Lucy Went to Buy a Hat by Alice Low, illustrated by Laura Huliska-Beith (HarperCollins, 2004)

Bad Cat Puts on His Top Hat by Tracy-Lee McGuinness-Kelly (Little Brown, 2005)

Casey's New Hat by Tricia Gardella, illustrated by Margot Apple (Houghton Mifflin, 1997)

The Cat in the Hat by Dr. Seuss (Random House, 1985)

Dog and Cat Shake a Leg [story "The Hat"] by Kate Spohn (Viking, 1996)

Follow That Hat by Pierre Pratt, illustrated by Geraldo Valerio (Annick Press, 1992)

Harry's Hats by Ann Tompert, illustrated by Marcelo Elizalde (Children's Press, 2004)

The Hat by Holly Keller (Harcourt, 2005)

A Hat for Ivan by Max Lucado, illustrated by David Wenzel (Crossway, 2004)

Hats! by Mem Fox, illustrated by Tricia Tusa (Harcourt, 2002)

Hats! by Margaret Nash, illustrated by Martin Impey (Sea-to-Sea, 2006)

Jennie's Hat by Ezra Jack Keats (Viking, 2003)

Kathy's Hats: A Story of Hope by Trudy Krisher (Albert Whitman, 1992)

Milo's Hat Trick by Jon Agee (Hyperion Books for Children, 2001)

Mrs. Honey's Hat by Pam Adams (Child's Play, 1990)

The Naughty Puppy by Jillian Powell, illustrated by Summer Durantz (Picture Window Books, 2003)

The Old Blue Hat by Dev Ross, illustrated by Meredith Johnson (Treasure Bay, 2001)

Old Hat, New Hat by Stan and Jan Berenstain (Random House, 1970)

Rembrandt's Hat by Susan Blackaby, illustrated by Mary Newell De Palma (Houghton Mifflin, 2002)

Shall I Knit You a Hat? by Kate Klise, M. Sarah Klise (Henry Holt, 2004)

Sherman Crunchley by Laura Joffe Numeroff and Nate Evans, illustrated by Tim Bowens (Dutton Children's Books, 2003)

What a Hat! by Holly Keller (Greenwillow Books, 2003)

Where's Mary's Hat? by Stephane Barroux (Viking, 2003)

Which Would You Rather Be? by William Steig, illustrated by Harry Bliss (Joanna Cotler Books, 2002)

Songs and Rhymes:

Crocodile Smile: 10 Songs ["I Am Not a Hat"] by Sarah Weeks, illustrated by Lois Ehlert (Geringer Books, 2003)

A Frog Inside My Hat: A First Book of Poems edited by Fay Robinson, illustrated by Cyd Moore (Troll Medallion, 1993)

PROJECT TWO: *My Hands*

 Relevance

As noted previously, children in the early childhood years need hands-on experience. Thus, no topic is more relevant to these early learners than what they can do with their hands. Initial preparation for a project on hands can begin with learning fingerplays in the library.

 Discussion

This experience will raise interest in a discussion about how we can use our fingers. Finger puppets and hand puppets can build on this experience of play involving hands. Children should have an opportunity to continue to explore using finger and hand puppets back in the classroom in their dramatic play area.

Children learn to turn pages of books in the library at this age. Beginning with board books and moving on to regular picture books will integrate this essential skill with a meaningful project about hands. This can lead to a further discussion about how we treat our books.

 Investigation

Back in the classroom, the teacher can ask the children to name all of the things that they do all day with their hands. The resulting notes and drawings on a poster called "Our Hands" will provide focus to the investigation stage of the project. Experts can be brought in to demonstrate a skill using their hands. Informative stories and nonfiction can be read in the classroom and library that will get the children talking about ways they use their hands. *A First Look at Touch* is a good choice to begin the exploration since it uses many key vocabulary words related to hands.

The possibilities for exploration and learning are limitless. Washing hands, putting things away, unbuttoning jackets, and practicing fine motor skills with age-appropriate manipulatives are all instances of how we use our hands. Through reading they will discover even more. Many of the nonfiction books about hands feature a page or two about sign language. If the children express an interest in this subject, a deaf person and an interpreter might visit the class to demonstrate how American Sign Language works. Children can easily be motivated to make an image of their hands. Ask the art teacher to show them how to use paint to make impressions of their hands on paper. These could be of use later in their final product. Music is another area that can easily integrate percussion and clapping into a unit about hands.

Readings in the library sessions that include information about touching and feeling objects can add a whole new dimension to their exploration as the children employ new vocabulary terms to describe what they are feeling as soft, furry, cold, or bumpy. Students might want to construct a feely box with the help of their teacher or place objects in a pillowcase for their friends to guess. These too can become part of the dramatic play area.

▶ End Product

Children can decide on the culmination of their project as their knowledge and experience grows. The end product might be a demonstration on all of the things that they can do with their hands. Children can choose to show their classmates one of the many activities that they have experienced over the course of the project.

Resources for "My Hands"

Informative Stories:

Hands by Dana Meachen Rau (Children's Press, 2000)

Hands: Growing Up to Be an Artist by Lois Ehlert (Harcourt, 2004 [new ed. of *Hands*, 1997])

Hands, Hands, Hands by Marcia K. Vaughan (Mondo Publishing, 1986)

My Father's Hands by Joanne Ryder (Morrow Junior Books, 1994)

Nonfiction:

26 Big Things Small Hands Do by Coleen Paratore (Free Spirit Publishing, 2004)

A to Z of Helping Hands by Tracy Maurer (Rourke, 2002)

Animal Touch by Kirsten Hall (Weekly Reader Early Learning Library, 2006)

Busy Fingers by C. W. Bowie, illustrated by Fred Willingham (Whispering Coyote, 2003)

Feeling Things by Allan Fowler (Children's Press, 1991)

Hands by Cynthia Fitterer Klingel (Weekly Reader Early Learning Library, 2002

Hands! by Virginia L. Kroll (Boyds Mills Press, 1997)

Hands by Simona Sideri (Smart Apple Media, 2005)

Hands Are Not for Hitting by Martine Agassi (Free Spirit Publishing, 2000)

Hands Can by Cheryl Willis Hudson (Candlewick Press, 2003)

Here Are My Hands by Bill Martin Jr. and John Archambault, illustrated by Ted Rand (Henry Holt, 1987)

I Touch with My Fingers by Joan Mills, illustrated by Peter Joyce (Schofield & Sims, 1986)

The Little Hands Art Book by Judy Press (Williamson, 1994)

Little Hands Create!: Art & Activities For Kids Ages 3 to 6 by Mary Doerfler Dall (Williamson, 2004)

My First Look at Touch (DK Publishing, 1990)

My Hands by Aliki (HarperCollins, 1990)

My Hands by Lloyd G. Douglas (Children's Press, 2004)

Paws and Claws by Elizabeth Miles (Heinemann Library, 2003)

Taking Care of My Hands and Feet by Terri Degezelle (Capstone Press, 2006)

Washing My Hands by Elizabeth Vogel (PowerKids Press, 2001)

Songs, Fingerplays, and Rhymes:

The Eentsy, Weentsy Spider: Fingerplays and Action Rhymes complied by Joanna Cole and Stephanie Calmensen, illustrated by Alan Tiegreen (Troll Associates, 1991)

If You're Happy and You Know It by Raffi (Knopf, 2005)

Little Hands Fingerplays & Action Songs: Seasonal Activities & Creative Play for 2- to 6-Year-Olds by Emily Stetson (Williamson, 2001)

PROJECT THREE: *Sounds All Around Us*

 ## Relevance

Some children at this age may not say much during discussions and readings, but they can be tempted to express themselves through sounds. Informative storybooks featuring the sounds of animals are plentiful, especially books that deal with animals on the farm, so this is a good candidate for collaboration between teacher and librarian. Children love to identify and practice these sounds, thus making this a relevant and engaging project idea for children. Stories, songs, and rhymes with onomatopoeia are appealing as well, as children imitate the sounds of honking cars, choo-chooing trains, or boo-hooing babies.

 ## Discussion

Class discussion for this project can begin with informative stories in classroom and library. Children can work on a poster with pictures of the various animals they are now able to imitate and identify by sound. Make a recording of the children as they make sounds according to pictures or actions mimed by the teacher. Children will enjoy identifying the sounds again when the recording is played back to them. This activity is also a good way to get children thinking about all the sounds they hear everyday.

 ## Investigation

An investigation into "Sounds in My World" can begin once children have started to make suggestions about all of the sounds they hear. An excursion or field trip to a familiar location such as the schoolyard, local zoo, or shopping center can get children listening for sounds. Ask children to predict what sounds they will hear before they begin their exploration. Parent volunteers and assistants can help children to record sounds that they identify when they are asked "What can you hear?" While working on their sound libraries, a visiting expert such as the school nurse can broaden the topic with a look at how we protect our ears. While hearing is a complex sense, basic information about ears and sound safety can be understood by young children. Children can be prepared for excursions and expert visits through exposure to related stories and information books in their library sessions. Keep track of all the sounds and other information that is explored during library classes so that it can be sent back to the classroom teacher at the end of every session.

Sounds are an obvious topic for music class, but art can incorporate the theme as well in paintings of big sounds (in bold stamps of color) and small sounds (using a brush to represent "quiet" sounds). No matter what the lesson, integrating sound can encourage students to vocalize, communicate, and listen.

▶ End Product

With the help of their teacher, students might decide to have as their end product a presentation or play about sounds in their world. Costumes and pictures are good cues to both performers and audience members in a performance about sound.

 ## Resources for "Sounds All Around Us"

Informative Stories:

"Buzz" Said the Bee by Wendy Cheyette Lewison, illustrated by Hans Wilhelm (Scholastic, 1992)

A Truck Goes Rattley-Bumpa by Jonathan London, illustrated by Denis Roche (Henry Holt, 2005)

All Sorts of Noises by Hannah Reidy, Illustrated by Emma Dodd (Picture Window, 2005)

Bark, George by Jules Feiffer (HarperCollins, 1999)

Barnyard Banter by Denise Fleming (Henry Holt, 1994)

Barnyard Song by Rhonda Gowler Greene, illustrated by Robert Bender (Atheneum Books for Young Readers, 1997)

Book! Book! Book! by Deborah Bruss, illustrated by Tiphanie Beeke (A.A. Levine, 2001)

Busy Little Mouse by Eugenie Fernandes, illustrated by Kim Fernandes, photography by Pat Lacroix (Kids Can Press, 2002)

Can You Choo Choo? by David Wojtowycz (Scholastic, 2003)

Can You Moo? by David Wojtowycz (Scholastic, 2003)

Choo Choo Clickety-Clack! by Margaret Mayo, Illustrated by Alex Ayliffe (Carolrhoda Books, 2004)

Cock-A-Moo-Moo by Juliet Dallas-Conte, illustrated by Alison Bartlett (Little, Brown, 2001)

Creepy Things Are Scaring Me by Jerome and Jarrett Pumphrey, illustrated by Rosanne Litzinger (HarperCollins, 2003)

Does a Cow Say Boo? by Judy Hindley, illustrated by Brita Granstrom (Candlewick Press, 2002)

Dog's Noisy Day: A Story to Read Aloud by Emma Dodd (Dutton Children's Books, 2002)

Down on the Farm by Merrily Kutner, illustrated by Will Hillenbrand (Holiday House, 2004)

Goodnight, Country by Susan Verlander (Chronicle Books, 2004)

Honk! by Mick Inkpen (Harcourt Brace, 1998)

Hoot! Hoot! by Richard Powell, illustrated by Ana Martin Larranaga (Candlewick Press, 2001)

I Heard a Little Baa by Elizabeth Macleod, illustrated by Louise Phillips (Kids Can Press, 1998)

In the City by Sheryl Mcfarlane, illustrated by Kim Lafave (Fitzhenry & Whiteside, 2004)

It Is the Wind by Ferida Wolff, illustrated by James Ransome (HarperCollins, 2005)

Listen To The Rain by Bill Martin, Jr. and John Archambault, illustrated by James Endicott (Henry Holt, 1988)

Look Who's Talking! At the Zoo by Danny Tepper, illustrated by Valeria Petrone (Random House, 2005)

Look Who's Talking! On the Farm by Danny Tepper, illustrated by Valeria Petrone (Random House, 2005)

Loud and Quiet, An Animal Opposites Book by Lisa Bullard (Capstone Press, 2006)

Max Found Two Sticks by Brian Pinkney (Aladdin Paperbacks, 1997)

Mice Squeak, We Speak: A Poem by Arnold L. Shapiro, illustrated by Tomie dePaola (Putnam, 1997)

Mommies Say Shhh! by Patricia Polacco (Philomel Books, 2005)

Moo Who? by Margie Palatini, illustrated by Keith Graves (Katherine Tegen Books, 2004)

Muncha, Muncha, Muncha by Candace Fleming, illustrated by Brian G. Karas (Atheneum Books for Young Readers, 2002)

Oink! Moo! How Do You Do?: A Book of Animal Sounds by Grace Maccarone, illustrated by Hans Wilhelm (Scholastic, 1994)

One Windy Wednesday by Phyllis Root, illustrated by Helen Craig (Candlewick Press, 1996)

Polar Bear, Polar Bear, What Do You Hear? by Bill Martin, Jr., illustrated by Eric Carle (Henry Holt, 1991)

Quiet Night by Marilyn Singer, illustrated by John Manders (Clarion Books, 2002)

Roar and More by Karla Kuskin (Boyds Mills Press, 1956 [new 2004 release])

Snow Music by Lynne Rae Perkins (Greenwillow Books, 2003)

Sounds of a Summer Night by May Garelick, illustrations by Candace Whitman (Mondo, 1991)

Spot Goes to the Farm by Eric Hill (Putnam, 1987)

Starry Safari by Linda Ashman, illustrated by Jeff Mack (Harcourt, 2005)

Tap! Tap! Tap! by Keith Faulner, illustrated by Jonathan Lambert (Barron's Educational, 2003)

The Baby Goes Beep by Rebecca O'Connell, Illustrated by Ken Wilson-Max (Roaring Brook Press, 2003)

The Cow That Went Oink by Bernard Most (Harcourt Brace, 1990)

The Day the Dog Said "Cock-a-Doodle Doo!" by David McPhail (Scholastic, 1997)

The Giraffe Who Cock-A-Doodle-Doo'd, A Pop-Up Book by Keith Faulkner, illustrated by Jonathan Lambert (Dial Books for Young Readers, 2001)

The Listening Walk by David Kirk Callaway (Viking Children's Books, 2005)

The Listening Walk by Paul Showers, illustrated by Aliki (HarperCollins, 1991)

The Noisy Way to Bed by Ian Whybrow, illustrated by Tiphanie Beeke (Arthur A. Levine, 2003)

The Seals on the Bus by Lenny Hort, illustrated by G. Brian Karas (Henry Holt, 2000)

The Very Noisy Night by Diana Hendry, illustrated by Jane Chapman (Dutton Children's Books, 1999)

This Little Chick by John Lawrence (Candlewick Press, 2002)

Vroomaloom Zoom by John Coy, illustrated by Joe Cepeda (Crown, 2000)

Wake Up, City by Susan Verlander (Chronicle Books, 2004)

What Shall We Do with the Boo-Hoo Baby? by Cressida Cowell, illustrated by Ingrid Codon (Scholastic, 2000)

What the Baby Hears by Laura Godwin, illustrated by Mary Morgan (Hyperion Books for Children, 2002)

Who Hoots? by Katie Davis (Harcourt, 2000)

Who Says Woof? by John Butler (Viking, 2003)

Nonfiction:

Do Bears Buzz? A Book about Animal Sounds by Michael Dahl, illustrated by Sandra D'Antonio (Picture Window Books, 2003)

Hearing by Claire Llewellyn (Sea to Sea, 2006)

Hearing by Sharon Gordon (Children's Press, 2001)

My Ears by Lloyd G. Douglas (Children's Press, 2004)

Shhhh—, A Book About Hearing by Dana Meachen Rau, illustrated by Rick Peterson (Picture Window Books, 2005)

So Many Sounds by Dana Meachen Rau, illustrated by Kristin Sorra (Children's Press, 2001)

Sound by Claire Llewellyn, photography by Ray Moller (Sea-to-Sea, 2005)

Sounds All Around by Wendy Pfeffer, illustrated by Holly Keller (HarperCollins, 1999)

Sounds All Around Us by Nancy Leber (Compass Point Books, 2004)

Songs and Rhymes:

Cat Goes Fiddle-I-Fee adapted and illustrated by Paul Galdone (Clarion, 1985)

Old Macdonald Had a Farm edited by Ann Owen, illustrated by Sandra D'Antonio (Picture Window Books, 2003)

The Seals on the Bus by Lenny Holt, illustrated by G. Brian Karas (Henry Holt, 2000)

PROJECT FOUR: *Babies*

 Relevance

Children of three years are proud of their growing independence and capabilities. Three-year-olds see themselves as very different from babies, but are nonetheless interested in these differences, especially those who have younger brothers or sisters at home. A discussion about babies will make it clear that this is a relevant topic for three-year-olds.

 Discussion

Children are often keen to talk about their younger siblings. This is a good jumping-off point for a project about babies. The discussion may begin with note-taking by the teacher on those students who have babies or expectant mothers at home. For those who don't, storybooks can provide both entertainment and information.

Many books about new babies focus on sibling rivalry. This project is more about babies themselves. What can they do? What do they need? How do parents look after babies? Children can offer their opinions and comments during the early stages of the project. Stories and nonfiction books will confirm and expand their knowledge and observations.

 Investigation

An investigation into babyhood can be greatly assisted by a "baby's room" dramatic play area. Children can use realistic dolls to role-play what they have learned about baby care. The children can decide on what supplies are needed to stock the baby room. Parents can be invited to provide items such as soothers, diapers, wipes, and plastic bottles. Once children are knowledgeable enough about the proper way to treat babies, it is time for an excursion or visit. A local hospital's maternity ward is a good place to learn about newborns from nurses, doctors, and new parents. Back in the classroom, parents can answer questions about some of the characteristics and needs of older babies. Both mothers and fathers should demonstrate parenting skills so that both boys and girls will be engaged with the materials in the dramatic play area.

 End Product

The end product of this investigation can be the baby's room itself. If students are involved in the planning and building of this site and use their new knowledge to create realistic scenes there, it will be clear that learning has taken place.

Resources for "Babies"

Informative Stories:

Babies by Ros Asquith, illustrated by Sam Williams (Simon & Schuster Books for Young Readers, 2003)

Bittle by Patricia MacLachlan and Emily MacLachlan, illustrated by Dan Yaccarino (HarperCollins, 2004)

Everywhere Babies by Susan Meyers, illustrated by Marla Frazee (Harcourt, 2001)

Froggy's Baby Sister by Jonathan London, illustrated by Frank Remkiewicz (Viking, 2003)

I Used to Be a Baby by Robin Ballard (Greenwillow, 2002)

Mommy Loves Her Baby; Daddy Loves His Baby by Tara Jaye Morrow, illustrated by Tiphanie Beeke (HarperCollins, 2003)

Now We Have a Baby by Lois Rock, illustrated by Jane Massey (Good Books, 2004)

Some Babies by Amy Schwartz (Orchard, 2000)

Star Baby by Margaret O'Hair, illustrated by Erin Eitter Kono (Clarion Books, 2005)

The Baby Goes Beep by Rebecca O'Connell, illustrated by Ken Wilson-Max (Roaring Brook Press, 2003)

The Day the Babies Crawled Away by Peggy Rathmann (G.P. Putnam's Sons, 2003)

The New Baby by Mary Packard, illustrated by Amanda Haley (Children's Press, 2004)

We Have a Baby by Cathryn Falwell (Clarion Books, 1993)

What Shall We Do with the Boo-Hoo Baby? by Cressida Cowell, illustrated by Ingrid Codon (Scholastic, 2000)

What the No-good Baby is Good For by Elise Broach, illustrated by Abby Carter (G. P. Putnam's Sons, 2005)

What's in Baby's Morning? by Judy Hindley, illustrated by Jo Burroughes (Candlewick Press, 2004)

When I Am a Sister by Robin Ballard (Greenwillow, 1998)

Nonfiction:

A Baby's Coming to Your House! by Shelley Moore Thomas, photographs by Eric Futran (Albert Whitman, 2001)

A Ride on Mother's Back: A Day Of Baby-Carrying Around The World by Emery Bernhard, illustrated by Durga Bernhard (Harcourt Brace, 1996)

Baby Faces by Margaret Miller (Little Simon, 1998)

Baby on the Way by William Sears, Martha Sears, and Christie Watts Kelly, illustrated by Renee Andriani (Little, Brown, 2001)

Baby Science: How Babies Really Work! by Ann Douglas, illustrated by Helene Desputeaux (Firefly Books, 1998)

Before You Were Born by Jennifer Davis, illustrated by Laura Cornell (Workman Publishing, 1997)

First Brother or Sister by Monica Hughes (Raintree, 2004)

Love That Baby!: A Book about Babies for New Brothers, Sisters, Cousins, and Friends by Kathryn Lasky, illustrated by Jennifer Plecas (Candlewick Press, 2004)

Mommy's in the Hospital Having a Baby by Maxine B. Rosenberg, photographs by Robert Maass (Clarion Books, 1997)

Supermom by Mick Manning, illustrated by Brita Granstrom (Albert Whitman, 1999)

The New Baby at Your House by Joanna Cole, photographs by Hella Hammid (Mulberry Books, 1985)

The New Baby by Fred Rogers, photographs by Jim Judkis (Penguin Putnam Books for Young Readers, 1985)

Welcoming Babies by Margy Burns Knight, illustrated by Anne Sibley O'Brien (Tilbury House, 1998)

What Baby Needs by William Sears, Martha Sears, and Christie Watts Kelly, illustrated by Renee Andriani (Little, Brown, 2001)

Songs and Poems:

Daddy-o Daddy!: Rare Family Songs of Woody Guthrie [sound recording] (Rounder Records Corp., 2001)

New Baby Train by Woody Guthrie, illustrated by Marla Frazee (Little, Brown, 1999)

Who's That Baby?: New-Baby Songs by Sharon Creech, illustrated by David Diaz (Joanna Cotler Books, 2005)

Chapter Four

Research and Inquiry in Pre-Kindergarten

Working With Children in Pre-Kindergarten

Four-year-old children are making great progress in their development of skills and knowledge of the world. According to the NAEYC's guide to developmentally appropriate practice, children at age four can do much more than they could just one year ago. Their fine motor development has improved so that they enjoy using scissors and can draw objects that are "recognizable to adults" since their drawings are now representational (Bredekamp and Copple 105; Malley). Shape, color, and size are familiar concepts. Malley would add basic concepts such as number, weight, texture, distance, time, and position to this list.

Children in pre-kindergarten often show an awareness of letters and an interest in writing and written texts. For instance, children at this age will start to point out letters that match the first letter in their name or the name of their friends. Four-year-olds will try – and some will succeed – at writing their names. Children will recognize some words by sight. However, the NAEYC warns against trying to drill students in the alphabet, phonics, and handwriting. What is important at this age is that the children are learning in a "print-rich environment that stimulates the development of language and literacy skills in a meaningful context" (Bredekamp 6). Of course, this is precisely what the project approach is all about.

Four-year-olds will begin to form and maintain friendships. Many will show a preference for working with certain children. However, others may still lack the social competencies to work with others. The teacher or librarian must support their efforts and teach them appropriate ways to convince others to work with them. Children may not have learned formulas for entering groups in a cooperative way, such as asking "May I help you?" or "May I join your group?" While some four-year-olds will have already mastered many of these social skills, others will need scaffolding from a supportive adult.

By pre-kindergarten, children's interests will have expanded beyond the family and home focus of preschool children. Thus the NAEYC recommends that the curriculum can broaden out to include excursions and field trips (Bredekamp 6). Thus the scope of potential topics for projects is much larger than in preschool.

By the time they reach four years of age, children can run around without banging into things. Their body/spatial awareness is now very good. Their temporal awareness has also improved since preschool. Four-year-olds are likely to notice if some part of their daily routine is skipped. Regular routines provide them with a sense of structure and security. Simple rules and clear guidelines to acceptable behavior are readily understood and even appreciated by children at this age (Driscoll and Nagel 48-49). These children enjoy asserting their independence. Allow them to try to do things for themselves. Step in to help only if children request help with shoes, belt buckles, and the like.

Four-year-olds have made great strides cognitively as well. It is common for children at this age to know if something in a story is real or pretend. Their ability to concentrate is longer than that of three-year-olds. Their memories are better. Memory strategies such as self-talk are used by four-year-olds. Gender may not yet be clear to them and their sense of right and wrong is still developing (Feiler and Tomonari 277). These children are still learning how to share and take turns, but adults can help them to develop this social competence by using a talking ball, by guiding them in playing games with rules, and by assisting them in making positive decisions to resolve conflicts when problems arise (Malley).

Four-year-olds like to ask "Why?" As Driscoll and Nagel note, "this is a time of extensive 'Why?' questions" (50). Malley describes four-year-olds as talkative people who enjoy serious discussions. She too notes that they ask many, many questions, especially about "How?" and "Why?"

The preschool years are a time for laughter and play, both with objects and words. Four-year-olds love to make jokes. Children will still laugh hilariously at their own jokes and those of their friends. Even when adults don't get the humor, it is still fun to join in their laughter and enjoyment of being silly.

Play is still very important for this age group, both outdoors and in a dramatic play area. As with three-year-olds, observing their behavior and listening to their invented scenarios at play can help teachers discover their preoccupations and interests. For instance, Malley notes that children of this age enjoy pretending to be "important adults." Thus, a project about adults and their jobs would be highly motivating as a topic for an extended project, as we shall see.

Informational Strategies in Pre-Kindergarten

In pre-kindergarten, the phonological awareness of children is growing. Letters of the alphabet are familiar to them. These children can recognize letters, especially those in their own name and those that begin the name of their friends. Strategies at this age can help to build knowledge and skills that will contribute to their development as researchers and inquirers.

Teachers and library media specialists can:

- demonstrate by pointing as they read that writing goes from left to right.
- focus on grapheme-phoneme correspondence in stories and nonfiction.
- demonstrate the conventions of English when reading – that print is read from top to bottom and from left to right.
- use e-book versions of stories and nonfiction to present large images of text to help children point out and comment on letters that they recognize.
- encourage children to practice "reading" (for themselves, their peers, or puppets).
- listen for comments during dialogic reading that can lead to authentic curriculum.
- answer questions that arise by turning to an informational book.
- note difficult questions for further investigation.
- read pictures and captions of an informational book.
- explicitly name captions as captions to raise children's awareness of what captions do.
- read labels that accompany pictures, diagrams, and photographs in informational books.
- refer to labels as labels.
- read only those pages from informational books that will help children explore their own current interests and questions (rather than reading books cover to cover).
- help children select books about subjects of interest to them.
- ask children to guess the contents of an informational book by the cover illustration.
- help children to label representative drawings.
- demonstrate the difference between drawing and writing when creating notes.
- ask children to show how to handle books and turn pages properly.
- ask children to articulate how they take care of books.
- prompt children to make connections between the content of books and their own experience.
- demonstrate that books can answer questions that arise during their exploration of objects and phenomenon.
- encourage children to use scribbling as writing.
- prompt children to answer questions about the events and characters in a story.
- prompt children to comment on phenomena depicted in nonfiction books.

Projects

PROJECT ONE: *Colors in My World*

 ## Relevance

Our brains love color and can distinguish hundreds of different shades. Colors are especially important to young children. Children are attracted to bright colors. Colors help children to identify and remember objects. Ask a young child to identify an object and he will probably name both the object and its color. Painting and drawing with colors are enjoyable and frequent activities for children at this age. By pre-kindergarten, children will even identify certain colors as their personal favorites. Color is an engaging and relevant topic for children at this age.

Not surprisingly, there are a vast number of children's books about colors – both stories and nonfiction. Usually written for children in the preschool years, they provide a wealth of print materials to enrich a project on colors.

A few simple texts can be used to start a class discussion of color. Most associate a color with a common animal or object. A perennial favorite is *Brown Bear, Brown Bear, What Do You See?*, which asks the bear (and the children) to identify animals and their colors. Other quick read-alouds that encourage children to identify colors in stories are *A Beach Ball Has Them All; Freight Train; Is It Red? Is It Yellow?: An Adventure in Color; Kipper's Book of Colors; Hello Kitty, Hello Color; One Gray Mouse; Maisy's Color Collection*, and *Dog's Colorful Day*. This last title has children identify the various spots Dog collects as he has mishap after mishap during a jaunt around the neighborhood. Children might want to create their own "colorful day" portraits after reading about Dog's day. Beginning with an outline of themselves on a large sheet of newsprint, children can then color different splashes of color on themselves to represent various spills they sometimes encounter.

Other possibilities are *Black Meets White*, a simple yet clever book about what happens when these two colors collide. *Bob's Vacation* follows a snowman as he travels to sunny climates to see more colors, but eventually returns to his arctic world with a few colorful accessories. *My Many Colored Days*, written but not illustrated by Dr. Seuss, is a beautiful and imaginative look at how colors can express our moods. *Leon the Chameleon* is a simple story about color with a powerful message: Being a different color does not make you any less a part of a community. Two other books that deal explicitly and well about different skin colors are *All the Colors of the Earth* by Sheila Hamanaka and *The Colors of Us* by Karen Katz.

 ## Discussion

The teacher and the librarian can plan to both get the discussion started with the many great fiction and informational books on this topic. For music class or a rollicking library class, children might also learn some songs and rhymes about color from *Wee Sing & Learn Colors* (a book and CD) or the book *Mary Wore Her Red Dress, and Henry Wore His Green Sneakers* (with musical score provided). This latter text can easily be altered to fit the clothes and names of students in the class.

Once children have had practice identifying colors and associating them with objects in their world, they may comment on their own favorite colors. A good story to get children talking about favorite colors is the story with photographs, *Chidi Only Likes Blue*, set in a colorful village in Nigeria. The librarian might get this started in library class – while wearing her own favorite color of course! The teacher could then follow-up by asking them if they would like to wear their favorite color to school the next day. Those who are interested should be encouraged to do so, with a note home to parents to help them find a piece of clothing to wear and talk about the next day.

It shouldn't take much effort to get children excited about a unit on colors. When children show up at school dressed in their favorite colors, this is an opportunity for the teacher to get them talking about colors and asking questions. Favorites can be noted on a colorful poster. Children can then rank the class favorites – what are the most popular colors? With the teacher's help, children can represent the results of this query on a bar graph or pictograph. What kinds of clothes have they worn? Children can name them and then classify them. What other objects come in these colors? This question opens up great potential for an exploration of items in the classroom and outside in the playground. A discussion of favorites will lead naturally to a discussion of colors in their world. Inevitably the children will start to think about the wider world, about explorations, and possible projects with tangible outcomes.

Another library link to this work in progress could be a nonfiction book about the color they have voted most popular (or least popular). The "Finding Colors" series by Moira Anderson, with each title bearing the name of a color (*Blue*, *Red*), the "Community of Color" series by Molly Dingles (*White as a Seashell*, *Blue as a Blueberry*), the "A+ Books – Colors" series by Michael Dahl (*Pink: Seeing Pink All Around Us*, *White: Seeing White All Around Us*) and Joanne Winne's series "The World of Color" (*Red in My World*, *Yellow in My World*) are good choices to get students thinking about real objects that they deal with every day. Other series on colors are listed in the resources section for this project.

Snack time and lunchtime can be another opportunity for the teacher to integrate a discussion of colors. Because Pre-K children usually eat in their classroom under the supervision of their teacher, it is a simple matter to introduce some healthy foods into their meals based on color. The librarian can help to prepare them for these discussions by reading children's informational books about foods and their colors. The Heinemann Library series "The Colors We Eat" covers this topic well.

Investigation

By this point, children will be ready to discuss ideas for further investigation. If they don't suggest it, prod them to consider an excursion around the school and its environs to look at all the different colors that they can identify. Timing may be important here. Depending on the climate, this project may be most appropriate at the beginning of the year when trees and flowers are in bloom. If there are a lot of deciduous trees on the school grounds, a fall setting might be interesting and there are plenty of books that look at the colors of autumn as well. Whatever the season, children will learn to use their powers of observation to discover more colors out there than they might have imagined.

Before the field trip, books about exploring the natural world for color could be shared with the children. Titles such as *City Colors*, *Brown as an Acorn*, *Beautiful Moments in the Wild: Animals and Their Colors*, or *What Color is Nature?* are good choices that will get children predicting what objects and animals they are likely to see in their neighborhood. The children can decide beforehand what kind of objects can be collected and safely brought back to the class.

Sightings of birds, squirrels, or other living creatures would be better captured on digital camera by the teacher and parent volunteers. Children could carry clipboards and try to draw objects with colored markers or pencils brought along by the adults. Or children might create a checklist of colors that they would check off as they identified an object or animal of each color. Teachers and parents should help scribe the names for these sightings. Of course, leaves, common wildflowers, sticks, and rocks could be collected and brought back to the classroom. It makes for an interesting class discussion to decide what flowers or living things can be picked beforehand. Of course, the environment around the school need not be limited to nature. Cars in the school parking lot, signs on the road, the flag, the school colors, recycling bins, and playground equipment can all be explored for colors.

Once all of this data is collected, ideas for projects may begin to emerge. Children might become very interested in classifying the colorful things that they have observed on their outing. Objects of the same color can be pulled together into an exhibit for parents, other students, and teachers to view. Students could act as helpers and guides to lead visitors around and help answer questions.

▶ End Product

As they develop their ideas about the end product, their investigation can continue. An expert such as the art teacher or a local artist could visit the class to demonstrate how primary colors can be mixed to create new secondary colors. Children should be given an opportunity to try this themselves with some red, blue, and yellow tempera paint. This experimentation can be followed up by a dialogic reading of books about primary colors and mixing of colors. In *Mouse Paint* three mice discover pots of red, blue, and yellow paint and have fun with the results. *Little Blue, Little Yellow* is an informative story about what happens when blue and yellow mix, as is *The Big Blue Spot*.

Another idea for a media center visitor would be a photographer who has documented some colorful event such as a circus, a Chinese New Year, a Hindu celebration of Holi (where colors are literally thrown at people), a fireworks celebration, or the painting of a large mural. Whatever the event, the wonderful photographs in *Cirque Du Soleil: Parade of Colors* make a good preliminary or follow-up read-aloud.

As the children get a clearer idea of the final product they will make to bring together all of their explorations of color in their world, the teacher will need to provide a model to the children. For an open house or exhibit on "Color in My World," the teacher could model how to arrange a display of objects, photographs, and paintings on various colors. She could help students practice how to lead visitors around to the various displays and how to answer questions about their displays.

Integrating Standards

Although a project about color might appear to involve only the creative development standards related to artistic expression, this project integrates many indicators in content areas such as science, math, language, physical education, health, and social studies. All of the essential dispositions or approaches to learning are present as well. From counting Dog's colorful spots to graphing and sorting the results of their explorations of items in class and outdoors, important mathematics standards are dealt with. The NCTM's standards for number and operations (counting), algebra (sorting and classifying), data analysis (organizing data about objects), communications (discussing their findings), and representation (communicating their findings through a chart or graph) are all addressed.

Scientific development indicators from Georgia's content-area standards are practiced when the children ask questions about objects; use their senses to observe, classify, and learn about objects; and use language to describe their observations. Social studies is in evidence when the children identify similarities and differences among people and demonstrate a growing awareness and respect for other cultures. Georgia's literacy indicators are present as children listen to stories, respond to questions, repeat rhymes, discuss books, and handle books. Even health standards are met when the children discuss various healthy foods of different colors.

As with any project, standards relating to approaches to learning are clearly met. Children have had ample opportunity to exhibit curiosity, initiative, creativity, and problem-solving. These dispositions, along with standards related to social-emotional development, will be noted by the teacher and librarian at each stage of the project.

Resources for "Colors in My World"

Fiction:

A Beach Ball Has Them All by Linzi West (Frances Lincoln, 2005)

All the Colors of the Earth by Sheila Hamanaka (Mulberry, 1994)

Black Meets White by Justine Fontes, illustrated by Geoff Waring (Walker Books, 2005)

Bob's Vacation by Dana Meachen Rau (Children's Press, 1999)

Brown Bear, Brown Bear, What Do You See? by Bill Martin, Jr., illustrated by Eric Carle [newly illustrated edition] (Henry Holt, 1992)

Chidi Only Likes Blue by Ifeoma Onyefulu (Cobblehill Books, 1997)

Dog's Colorful Day: A Messy Story about Colors and Counting by Emma Dodd (Puffin Books, 2000)

Hello Kitty, Hello Color by Higashi Glaser (Harry N. Abrams, 2001)

Leon the Chameleon by Mélanie Watt (Kids Can Press, 2001)

Little Blue and Little Yellow by Leo Lionni (Mulberry, 1995)

Maisy's Color Collection by Lucy Cousins (Candlewick Press, 2005)

Mary Wore Her Red Dress, & Henry Wore His Green Sneakers adapted and illustrated by Merle Peek (Clarion, 1985)

Mouse Paint by Ellen Stoll Walsh (Harcourt Brace, 1989)

My Many Colored Days by Dr. Seuss, illustrated by Steve Johnson and Lou Fancher (Knopf, 1996)

One Gray Mouse by Katherine Burton, illustrated by Kim Fernandes (Kids Can Press, 1997)

The Big Blue Spot by Peter Holwitz (Philomel, 2003)

The Colors of Us by Karen Katz (Henry Holt, 1999)

Information Books:

Beautiful Moments in the Wild: Animals and Their Colors edited by Stephanie Maze (Moonstone Press, 2002)

Cirque Du Soleil: Parade of Colors by Patrisha Robertson (Abrams Books for Young Readers, 2003)

City Colors by Zoran Milich (Kids Can Press, 2004)

Freight Train by Donald Crews (Greenwillow, 1978)

Is It Red? Is It Yellow?: An Adventure In Color by Tana Hoban (Mulberry, 1978)

Kipper's Book of Colors by Mick Inkpen (Harcourt, 1995)

What Color is Nature? by Stephen R. Swinburne (Boyds Mills Press, 2002)

Informational Series:

"Colors" series:

Black: Seeing Black All Around Us by Michael Dahl (Capstone Press, 2005)

Brown: Seeing Brown All Around Us by Michael Dahl (Capstone Press, 2005)

Pink: Seeing Pink All Around Us by Michael Dahl (Capstone Press, 2005)

White: Seeing White All Around Us by Michael Dahl (Capstone Press, 2005)

"Community of Color" series:

Black as a Bat by Molly Dingles, illustrated by Walter Velez (Dingles & Co., 2004)

Blue as a Blueberry by Molly Dingles, illustrated by Walter Velez (Dingles & Co., 2004)

Brown as an Acorn by Molly Dingles, illustrated by Walter Velez (Dingles & Co., 2004)

Gray as a Dolphin by Molly Dingles, illustrated by Walter Velez (Dingles & Co., 2004)

Green as a Frog by Molly Dingles, illustrated by Walter Velez (Dingles & Co., 2003)

Orange as a Pumpkin by Molly Dingles, illustrated by Walter Velez (Dingles & Co., 2004)

Pink as a Piglet by Molly Dingles, illustrated by Walter Velez (Dingles & Co., 2004)

Purple as a Plum by Molly Dingles, illustrated by Walter Velez (Dingles & Co., 2004)

Red as a Fire Truck by Molly Dingles, illustrated by Walter Velez (Dingles & Co., 2004)

Turquoise as a Parakeet by Molly Dingles, illustrated by Walter Velez (Dingles & Co., 2005)

White as a Seagull by Molly Dingles, illustrated by Walter Velez (Dingles & Co., 2004)

Yellow as a Lemon by Molly Dingles, illustrated by Walter Velez (Dingles & Co., 2004)

"Finding Colors" series:

Blue by Moira Anderson (Heinemann, 2006)

Green by Moira Anderson (Heinemann, 2006)

Red by Moira Anderson (Heinemann, 2006)

Yellow by Moira Anderson (Heinemann, 2006)

"The Colors We Eat" series:

Black Foods by Isabel Thomas (Heinemann Library, 2005)

Blue and Purple Foods by Isabel Thomas (Heinemann Library, 2005)

Brown Foods by Patricia Whitehouse (Heinemann Library, 2002)

Food ABC by Patricia Whitehouse (Heinemann Library, 2002)

Green Foods by Patricia Whitehouse (Heinemann Library, 2002)

Orange Foods by Patricia Whitehouse (Heinemann Library, 2003)

Pink Foods by Isabel Thomas (Heinemann Library, 2005)

Red Foods by Patricia Whitehouse (Heinemann Library, 2002)

Sorting Foods by Patricia Whitehouse (Heinemann Library, 2002)

Yellow Foods by Patricia Whitehouse (Heinemann Library, 2002)

White Foods by Patricia Whitehouse (Heinemann Library, 2002)

"The World of Color" series:

Blue in My World by Joanne Winne (Children's Press, 2000)

Green in My World by Joanne Winne (Children's Press, 2000)

Orange in My World by Joanne Winne (Children's Press, 2000)

Red in My World by Joanne Winne (Children's Press, 2000)

White in My World by Joanne Winne (Children's Press, 2000)

Yellow in My World by Joanne Winne (Children's Press, 2000)

Other Nonfiction Books:

A First Book about Colors by Nicola Tuxworth (Gareth Stevens, 1999)

All about Color by Irene Bates, illustrated by Jill Newton (Thameside Press, 2002)

Blue by Lisa Bruce (Raintree, 2004)

Blue by Sarah L. Schuette (A+ Books, 2003)

Can You See the Red Balloon? by Stella Blackstone, illustrated by Debbie Harter (Orchard Books, 1998)

Changing Colour by Joy Richardson (Franklin Watts, 1997)

Color Zoo by Lois Ehlert. (Lippincott, 1989)

Colors by Alvin Granowsky (Copper Beach Books, 2001)

Colors by Roger Pare (Gareth Stevens, 2001)

Colors Everywhere by Tana Hoban (Greenwillow Books, 1995)

Colors with Tropical Animals by Mélanie Watt (Kids Can Press, 2005)

Green by Lisa Bruce (Raintree, 2004)

Green by Sarah L. Schuette (A+ Books, 2003)

Look! by Kyra Teis (Star Bright Books, 2005)

My Very First Book of Colors by Eric Carle (Philomel Books, 1974)

My Very First Look at Colors by Christiane Gunzi (Two Can, 2001)

Orange by Sarah L. Schuette (A+ Books, 2003)

Purple by Sarah L. Schuette (A+ Books, 2003)

Red by Lisa Bruce (Raintree, 2004)

Red by Sarah L. Schuette (A+ Books, 2003))

Red, Blue, Color Zoo by Philippe Dupasquier (Candlewick Press, 2002)

Red, Blue, Which Color Are You? by Philippe Dupasquier (Walker, 2002)

Strawberries Are Red by Petr Horácek (Walker, 2001)

Yellow by Lisa Bruce (Raintree, 2004)

Yellow by Mary Elizabeth Salzmann (SandCastle, 2000)

Wee Sing & Learn Colors by Pamela Beall and Susan Nipp, illustrated by Pongmee Yudthana (Price Stern Sloan, 2000)

Yoyo's Colors by Jeannette Rowe (Tiger Tales, 2002)

Zoe's Hats: A Book of Colors and Patterns by Sharon Lane Holm (Boyds Mills Press, 2003)

PROJECT TWO: *What's the Weather Like in Springtime?*

 ## Relevance

A good early approach to scientific observation and learning is to examine the weather. Spring is a good time to experience a variety of weather patterns: sunshine and rain; clear skies and clouds; windy days and gentle breezes; warm days and cold. Four-year-olds are capable of noting types of weather and making simple measurements. Being properly dressed for the weather is important to young children because they enjoy playing outdoors. A project that focuses on becoming more knowledgeable about the weather is a relevant and motivating topic.

 ## Discussion

Children can be brought into a conversation about weather through stories that center on people or animals and what they do in different kinds of weather. This initial discussion will bring weather words to the front. As new words or useful words come up, the teacher and librarian can add them to their project vocabulary list. Because these words describe physical phenomena it is easy to pair the words with concrete images that the children can then refer to throughout the life of the project. Children enjoy sharing their experiences of rainy days, windy days, or sunny days. Categorizing their responses under weather symbols is a good start to a project about spring weather.

 ## Investigation

As an investigation of weather gets underway, children will decide what kinds of observations they will attempt to make. Can they remember what the weather was like yesterday? Placing a weather symbol on the class calendar will get them thinking about the other kinds of weather information that they could measure and take note of. Are there clouds in the sky? Are they white or gray or black? Why? Is it windy? Is it raining? How much rain is falling? How can we tell? Many questions and ideas will be raised about how they can organize themselves to do a thorough examination of springtime weather.

 ## End Product

Children can examine weather reports in the local newspaper and compare this information to their own observations. The symbols and notations used may give the children ideas about how they can present information about springtime weather in an end product. When their observations over a period of weeks in the spring are complete, they will be ready to present their findings. Groups of children can explain how they took notations and what they can say about the amount of sun, rain, clouds, and wind that are typical of springtime in their region. Later on, in grade two, this topic can be revisited in a more abstract way as children examine how people try to predict weather patterns.

 ## Resources for "What's the Weather Like in Springtime?"

Informational Stories:

Bright and Breezy by Alan Rogers (World Book/Two-Can, 1998)

Cloudy Day, Sunny Day by Donald Crews (Harcourt Brace, 1999)

Days of the Week by Terri Dougherty, illustrated by Justin Greathouse (Picture Window Books, 2005)

Hello, Sun! by Dayle Ann Dodds, illustrated by Sachiko Yoshikawa (Dial Books for Young Readers, 2005)

Maisy's Wonderful Weather Book by Lucy Cousins (Candlewick Press, 2006)

Moe McTooth: An Alley Cat's Tale by Eileen Spinelli, illustrated by Linda Bronson (Clarion Books, 2003)

Nana's Cold Days by Adwoa Badoe, illustrated by Bushra Junaid (Douglas & McIntyre, 2002)

Otto's Rainy Day by Natasha Yim, illustrated by Pamela R. Levy (Charlesbridge, 2000)

Rain and Shine by Deborah Kespert and Sue Barraclough, illustrated by Fran Jordan (Two Can, 2000)

Sail Away by Donald Crews (HarperTrophy, 1995)

Some Things Change by Mary Murphy (Houghton Mifflin, 2001)

Splosh! by Mick Inkpen (Harcourt Brace, 1998)

Sunny Sunday Drive by Janine Scott, illustrated by Ian Forss (Picture Window Books, 2005)

The Aunts Go Marching by Maurie J. Manning (Boyds Mills Press, 2003)

The Mole Sisters and the Rainy Day by Roslyn Schwartz (Annick Press, 1999)

The Weather by Olivia George, illustrated by Rusty Fletcher (Children's Press, 2005)

Think Cool Thoughts by Elizabeth Perry, illustrated by Linda Bronson (Clarion, 2005)

Information Books:

A Rainy Day by Lola M. Schaefer (Capstone Press, 2000)

A Rainy Day by Robin Nelson (Lerner, 2002)

A Sunny Day by Lola M. Schaefer (Capstone Press, 2000)

A Sunny Day by Robin Nelson (Lerner, 2002)

Cloudy Days by Jennifer S. Burke (Children's Press, 2000)

Cold Days by Jennifer S. Burke (Children's Press, 2000)

Fun with the Sun by Melissa Stewart (Compass Point Books, 2004)

Hot Days by Jennifer S. Burke (Children's Press, 2000)

It Is Raining by Kelly Doudna (Abdo Publishing, 2003)

It Is Sunny by Kelly Doudna (Abdo Publishing, 2003)

It's Raining! by Julie Richards (Smart Apple Media, 2005)

It's Sunny! by Julie Richards (Smart Apple Media, 2004)

Rainy Days by Jennifer S. Burke (Children's Press, 2000)

Sunny Days by Jennifer S. Burke (Children's Press, 2000)

The Rainy Day Book by Jane Bull (DK Publishing, 2003)

The Sunny Day Book by Jane Bull (DK Publishing, 2004)

Weather by Alice K. Flanagan (Compass Point Books, 2000)

Whatever the Weather by Karen Wallace, illustrated by Gill Tomblin (DK Publishing, 1999)

What's the Weather Today? by Allan Fowler (Children's Press, 1991)

Windy Days by Jennifer S. Burke (Children's Press, 2000)

Songs and Rhymes:

Anna Moo Crackers [sound recording] by Anna Moo (A. Moosic Productions, 1994, [includes "Sunny, Sunny Day"])

It's Raining, It's Pouring by Kin Eagle, illustrated by Rob Gilbert (Gareth Stevens, 1996)

Video/DVD:

Rainy Day Recess [videorecording] (100% Educational, 1999, 11 min.)

PROJECT THREE: *Taste and Smell*

 ## Relevance

Children have sensitive taste buds, which is why they are sometimes fussy eaters. But it also means that they are good at sensing particular tastes and smells. Increasing their vocabulary of particular taste sensations will help them to describe what their preferences are when it comes to food and drink. Children of this age enjoy helping to prepare snacks and lunches, making this project relevant and engaging.

 ## Discussion

By the time children are four, they have definite food likes and dislikes. Getting an initial listing of favorite foods and drinks will be the foundation of the experimentation to follow. Kid-friendly books about favorite and not-so-favorite foods, plus funny stories about bad smells are a good approach to discussion in the library. As project-related comments or questions are made, they should be noted by the librarian and added to the materials for the classroom investigation.

 ## Investigation

The teacher can lead children through some initial experimentation to identify the basic kinds of tastes: sweet, salty, sour, and bitter. Nonfiction books that show a "map" of these tastes on the human tongue can be understood by children of this age. Though magnified images of taste buds will not make sense to most four-year-olds, the term is useful when asking them – "What are your taste buds telling you?"

Library periods can be used to build knowledge and terminology that will further their efforts at direct exploration in the classroom. Begin with some humorous stories involving taste and smell. Hally Tosis and Dirk, those two smelly dogs, can get children talking about good and bad smells or their own experiences with pet dogs. These stories may raise questions about a dog's sense of smell or about why some things smell bad. Answers can readily be found in the library's nonfiction section. Fanciful stories such as *My Little Sister Ate One Hare* might be used to have the children invent their own story of a child who eats some impossible objects. The investigation can then move on to realistic stories such as Lauren Child's book about a fussy eater. Children are sure to relate to this book and to want to discuss their food likes and dislikes. As usual, notes from this discussion can then be taken back to the class for math activities involving sorting and classifying or creating charts and graphs.

A classroom chart categorizing foods and drinks by the four taste descriptors can be made up of images and words. Children can devise blindfold tests of foods to smell. Can their classmates identify foods and drinks by smell alone? By the time children are four or five, they can sort information about objects by more than one attribute (Bredekamp and Copple, 113). Student preferences and dislikes can be noted. Substances such as sour lemon juice may be altered by the simple addition of sugar into a palatable drink of lemonade. Hands-on experiences stirring liquids, pouring drinks, building sandwiches, and setting out pieces of fruit will make this project both enjoyable and memorable.

As experiments and investigations in the classroom develop, the library sessions can move from fiction to nonfiction sources. Questions that arise in class can be answered. Dialogic readings of nonfiction can help increase the children's vocabulary related to their senses and raise new questions.

▶ End Product

The end product for an inquiry into taste and smell will probably involve direct experience of food and drink. Assisted by their charts and notations, children may design a snack for another class or some visiting teachers or parents. At each table small groups can explain what tastes and smells are being presented and what the class has learned about them.

Resources for "Taste and Smell"

Stories:

A Taste for Noah by Susan Remick Topek, illustrated by Sally Springer (Kar-Ben Copies, 1993)

Benny by Sieb Posthuma (Miller Book Publishers, 2003)

Bon Appetit!: Musical Food Fun [sound recording] by Cathy Fink and Marcy Marxer (Rounder Kids, 2003)

Bread and Jam for Frances by Russell Hoban, illustrated by Lillian Hoban [newly illustrated edition] (HarperCollins, 1992)

Dog Breath: The Horrible Trouble with Hally Tosis by Dav Pilkey (Blue Sky Press, 1994)

I Will Never Not Ever Eat a Tomato by Lauren Child (Candlewick Press, 2000)

King Smelly Feet by Hiawyn Oram, illustrated by John Shelley (Andersen Press, 2002)

Lima's Red Hot Chilli by David Mills, illustrated by Derek Brazell, Gujarati translation by Bhadra Patel (Mantra, 2000)

Livingstone Mouse by Pamela Duncan Edwards, illustrated by Henry Cole (HarperCollins, 1996)

Mouse Mess by Linnea Riley (Blue Sky Press, 1997)

Mr. Blewitt's Nose: Featuring Primrose Pumpkin, Her Helpful Nature & Her Incredibly Smelly Dog, Dirk by Alastair Taylor (Houghton Mifflin, 2005)

My Little Sister Ate One Hare by Bill Grossman, illustrated by Kevin Hawkes (Crown Publishers, 1996)

Peanut by Heidi Kilgras, illustrated by Mike Reed (Random House, 2003)

Sweet Tooth by Margie Palatini, illustrated by Jack E. Davis (Simon and Schuster Books for Young Readers, 2004)

The Nose Knows by Ellen Weiss, illustrated by Margeaux Lucas (Kane Press, 2002)

The Very Hungry Caterpillar by Eric Carle (Philomel Books, 1987)

Yoko by Rosemary Wells (Hyperion Books for Children, 1998)

Information Books:

Eating by Claire Llewellyn (Smart Apple Media, 2005)

Eating by Gwenyth Swain (Carolrhoda Books, 1999)

Eating the Alphabet: Fruits and Vegetables from A to Z by Lois Ehlert (Harcourt Brace, 1989)

I Eat Vegetables! by Hannah Tofts, photographs by Rupert Horrox (Zero to Ten, 1998)

My Mouth by Lloyd G. Douglas (Children's Press, 2004)

My Nose by Kathy Furgang (PowerKids Press, 2001)

My Nose by Lloyd G. Douglas (Children's Press, 2004)

Sense of Taste by Carey Molter (Abdo Publishing, 2001)

Smell by Sue Hurwitz, photographs by Seth Dinnerman (PowerKids Press, 1997)

Smell: A True Book by Patricia J. Murphy (Children's Press, 2003)

Smelling and Tasting by Claire Llewellyn (Sea to Sea, 2005)

Smelling and Tasting by Lillian Wright (Raintree Steck-Vaughn, 1995)

Smelling by Helen Frost (Capstone Press, 2000)

Smelling by Kimberley Jane Pryor (Chelsea Clubhouse, 2003)

Smelling by Rebecca Olien (Capstone Press, 2006)

Smelling by Sharon Gordon (Children's Press, 2001)

Smelling in Living Things by Karen Hartley, Chris Macro, and Philip Taylor, illustrated by Alan Fraser (Heinemann Library, 2000)

Smelling Things by Allan Fowler (Children's Press, 1991)

Taste by Angela Royston (Smart Apple Media, 2005)

Taste by Kay Woodward (Gareth Stevens, 2005)

Taste by Maria Hidalgo (Smart Apple Media, 2004)

Taste by Maria Rius, illustrated by J.M. Parramon, J.J. Puig (Barrons, 1983)

Taste by Sue Hurwitz (PowerKids Press, 1997)

Taste: A True Book by Patricia J. Murphy (Children's Press, 2003)

Tastes Good! by Sally Hewitt (QEB Pub., 2005)

Tasting by Helen Frost (Pebble Books/Capstone Press, 2000)

Tasting by Kimberley Jane Pryor (Chelsea Clubhouse Books, 2003)

Tasting by Rebecca Olien (Capstone Press, 2006)

Tasting by Sharon Gordon, illustrated by Patricia Rasch (Children's Press, 2001)

Tasting in Living Things by Karen Hartley, Chris Macro, and Philip Taylor, illustrated by Alan Fraser (Heinemann Library, 2000)

Tasting Things by Allan Fowler, images supplied by VALAN photos (Children's Press, 1991)

What Can I Taste? (Raintree, 2005)

You Can't Smell a Flower with Your Ear by Joanna Cole (Grosset & Dunlap, 1994)

Yum!: A Book about Taste by Dana Meachen Rau, illustrated by Rick Peterson (Picture Window Books, 2005)

PROJECT FOUR: *Doctors and Nurses*

 ## Relevance

Most schools have a resident or visiting doctor or nurse. These people are key experts in an investigation into the career and daily functions of a general practitioner of medicine. An inquiry into the work of a medical professional is relevant to children who enjoy pretending to be adults at work. This project has the added benefit of introducing both the person and the treatments that are part of a typical visit to the school nurse or doctor. A project such as this can go a long way to reducing anxiety that some children may feel about the doctor's office.

 ## Discussion

Most children will have had some experience at a doctor's office or hospital already. Sharing their ideas and experiences at the beginning of this project will expose any misconceptions that they might have and that the project itself will rectify. Children may already have a fairly good inventory of medical terms in their vocabulary. Now is the time to find out. Reading stories that are both fun and informative will assist the discussion process.

 ## Investigation

Children will find the idea of building a medical office of their own an exciting proposition. There will be a lot to plan and think about. What equipment will they need? Should they have realistic dolls as patients? How will they dress? What procedures or treatments will they provide in their clinic? Nonfiction books that describe what doctors and nurses do will help develop their ideas. Once they have prepared a tentative listing with the help of their teacher and librarian, they are ready to continue their investigation with a visit to their school nurse or doctor.

 ## End Product

Dramatic play areas are ideal settings in which to integrate curriculum goals in numeracy and literacy, and thus make a good end product for a unit on doctors and nurses. Wall charts for measuring height, scales for weighing, inventories of band-aids and other supplies, files for patients, and labels for various equipment all add to a rich environment of print and numbers. This area can be used for role plays for the class as a whole and individual dramatic play during playtimes.

Resources for "Doctors and Nurses"

Fun Stories:

Doctor De Soto by William Steig (Farrar, Straus, And Giroux, 1982)

Doctor Me Di Cin by Roberto Piumini, illustrated by Piet Grobler (Front Street, 2001)

Dr. Dog by Babette Cole (Dragonfly Books, 1994)

Dr. Duck and the New Babies by H.M. Ehrlich, illustrated by Laura Rader (Blue Apple Books, 2005)

Froggy Goes to the Doctor by Jonathan London, illustrated by Frank Remkiewicz (Viking, 2002)

Help! by Christopher Inns (Frances Lincoln, 2004)

Mother Mother I Feel Sick, Send for the Doctor Quick Quick Quick by Remy Charlip and Burton Supree, illustrated by Remy Charlip (Tricycle Press, 2001)

Next Please by Ernst Jandl, illustrated by Norman Junge (G.P. Putnam's Sons, 2003)

Informative Stories:

Betty's Not Well Today by Gus Clarke (Andersen/Trafalgar, 2003)

Doctor Maisy by Lucy Cousins, illustrated by King Rollo Films Ltd. (Candlewick, 2001)

Dress-Up by Marcia Leonard, photographs by Dorothy Handelman (Millbrook Press, 1999)

Felix Feels Better by Rosemary Wells (Candlewick Press, 2001)

I Am Sick by Patricia Jensen, illustrated by Johanna Hantel (Children's Press, 2005)

My Friend the Doctor by Joanna Cole, illustrated by Maxie Chambliss (HarperCollins, 2005)

Shanna's Doctor Show by Jean Marzollo, illustrated by Shane W. Evans (Jump at the Sun/Hyperion Books for Children, 2001)

Time to See the Doctor by Heather Maisner, illustrated by Kristina Stephenson (Kingfisher, 2004)

Nonfiction:

A Day in the Life of a Doctor by Heather Adamson (Capstone Press, 2004)

A Day in the Life of a Doctor by Mary Bowman-Kruhm and Claudine G. Wirths (PowerKids Press, 1997)

A Day in the Life of a Doctor by Linda Hayward, photographs by Keith Harrelson (DK Publishing, 2001)

A Day in the Life of a Nurse by Liza N. Burby, photographs by Ethan Zindler (PowerKids Press, 1999)

A Day with a Doctor by Jan Kottke, photographs by Thaddeus Harden (Children's Press, 2000)

A Trip to the Doctor by Deborah Lock (DK Publishing, 2005)

Doctor by Heather Miller (Heinemann Library, 2003)

The Doctor's Office by B.A. Hoena (Capstone Press, 2004)

The Doctor's Office by Gail Saunders-Smith (Pebble Books, 1998)

Doctor Tools by Inez Snyder, photographs by Maura B. Mcconnell (Children's Press, 2002)

Doctors by Mary K. Dornhoffer (Compass Point Books, 2000)

Does a Hippo Say Ahh? by Fred Ehrlich, illustrated by Emily Bolam (Blue Apple Books, 2003)

Going to the Doctor by Anne Civadi, illustrated by Stephen Cartwright (Usborne, 2000)

Going to the Doctor by Ian Smith, photographs by Steve Lumb (QEB Pub., 2004)

Going to the Doctor by Melinda Beth Radabaugh (Heinemann Library, 2004)

I Want to Be a Doctor by Dan Liebman (Firefly Books, 2000)

I Want to Be a Doctor by Liza Alexander (Western Publishing Company, 1991)

Let's Talk about Going to the Doctor by Marianne Johnston (PowerKids Press, 1997)

Let's Talk about Having a Broken Bone by Elizabeth Weitzman (PowerKids Press, 1997)

Let's Talk about Having the Flu by Elizabeth Weitzman (PowerKids Press, 1997)

Let's Talk about Needing Glasses by Diane Shaughnessy (PowerKids Press, 1997)

What to Expect When You Go to the Doctor by Heidi Murkoff, illustrated by Laura Rader (HarperFestival, 2000)

Songs:

Miss Polly Has a Dolly retold by Pamela Duncan Edwards, illustrated by Elicia Castaldi (G.P. Putnam's Sons, 2003)

People in Our Neighborhood: Songs about Community Helpers and Workers [Sound Recording] by Ronno (Kimbo Educational, 1996 [includes "Doctor, Doctor!"])

Chapter Five

Research and Inquiry in Kindergarten

Working With Children in Kindergarten

Five-year-olds are embarking on another year of incredible progress, though their physical growth is now slower than in the previous two years. Driscoll and Nagel refer to years from five to eight as one of "spectacular cognitive growth in the ability to handle complex mental tasks" (53). Many of the skills that preschool and pre-kindergarten children were developing are now accomplished in the fifth year. Their body/spatial awareness is now very good. Their temporal awareness has developed to the point where they know how their day is structured and respond to bells ringing to mark the end of a class. Now very independent, five-year-olds need less help with personal tasks. Friendships are very important to them. Gender will be understood as a matter of physical anatomy, not how you dress or the length of your hair (Driscoll and Nagel 48-52).

Five-year-olds understand the difference between reality and fantasy. Children will inform their teacher or librarian about elements of a story that are make-believe. According to the NAEYC's guide to developmentally appropriate practice, most five-year-olds can "sort and classify using more than one attribute of an object (e.g., color and size)" (Bredekamp and Copple 113). Five-year-olds are now better at remembering things, and can be observed using mnemonics such as repeating a piece of information over and over again so that they will remember it (Driscoll and Nagel 53). Thus Lesia Oesterreich of Iowa State University's Human Development and Family Studies program notes that at five years children can memorize their phone number and address. These children can remember stories and retell them. They understand and use categories. Of special interest is the fact that they are "project-minded," enjoying plans, dramatic scenarios, and drawings.

The language skills of five-year-olds are now well developed. Most five-year-olds can speak sentences of between five and seven words, use the past tense, and tell familiar stories (Feiler & Tomonari 277). According to Oesterreich, children at this age understand about 13,000 words. According to the NAEYC, most five-year-olds show an interest in "the functional aspects of written language, such as recognizing meaningful words and trying to write their own names" (Bredekamp 6).

Like younger children, they are still working on sharing and taking turns, but they often succeed at these tasks. Concentration can be sustained for longer periods. Working in larger groups is possible when the topic is meaningful to them. These abilities make it possible to engage them in longer and more in-depth projects than ever before. Children at this age are eager to learn about the world. The NAEYC recommends that five-year-olds be taken to special events and field trips because of their "developing interest in community and the world outside their own" (Bredekamp 6). This is another factor that will affect the potential pool of topic ideas of interest to them.

Informational Strategies in Kindergarten

Kindergarten is a year of emerging literacy. Children recognize and learn to write their names. Five-year-olds will begin to recognize some words and use invented spelling to write. Many strategies support their developing literacy skills and its connection to informational strategies required for research. Thus, children:

- web current knowledge and note questions on a topic with the help of a teacher who scribes for them.
- recall and note knowledge gained from informative stories and nonfiction with the help of the teacher or librarian.
- use invented spelling, drawing, and photographs to document their observations during an excursion related to a project.
- can read captions that describe photographs in informational books.
- dictate captions to describe their own photographs during project work.
- point out words that they recognize in stories and early nonfiction books (especially on large projections of e-books).
- ask comprehension questions about nonfiction readings.
- "read" and discuss early nonfiction books in pairs.
- use highlighter tape to highlight words in early nonfiction books that they recognize.
- write one-word captions to accompany their drawings and photographs.

Projects

PROJECT ONE: *Signs All Around Us*

Relevance

By the time children are in kindergarten, they have begun to identify traffic lights and signs. The connection between print on signs or billboards and information about consumer products or community services is clear to them. For example, these children can identify signs for their favorite stores or restaurants and for places that they like to visit such as water parks or public libraries. Visual elements and special shapes and colors of many signs help even early emergent readers identify many of these signs with relative ease. Because of the interest children of this age are taking in signs, this is a good time to motivate children to begin this relevant project about "Signs All Around Us."

Surprisingly few storybooks deal specifically with signs. Thus, any storybooks that might be used to raise awareness of signs and increase vocabulary about this topic will have to be sought circumspectly, in narratives that just happen to include traffic signs and common commercial signs. Fortunately, a bit of rummaging around in the fiction stacks will reveal plenty of books that will draw children's attention to signs in their world.

Discussion

The easiest fiction picks for opening discussions are books about travel and traffic. These books don't deal directly with rules of the road, but they do explore situations that children have experienced themselves and feature pictures of road signs and traffic lights. A few examples are *Policeman Lou and Policewoman Sue* by Lisa Desimini, *Rush Hour* by Christine Loomis, and *School Bus* by Donald Crews. As well, *Don't Ever Cross That Road: An Armadillo Story* and *Rush Hour* are sure to get children talking about their experiences with crossing the street and city traffic.

Other storybooks feature signs in our community, above shops, in windows, on posters, and in school. Examples include the signs for neighborhood stores in *On the Town: A Community Adventure* and common mall signs in *The Awful Aardvarks Shop for School*. Even stories that have nothing in the title to suggest they can be good choices for this project may work. *Different, Just Like Me* features streetscapes with common kinds of shop signs. These introductory stories about common encounters with signs can be read during regular library periods and in the classroom.

Once the subject of signs has been raised, a discussion can begin about the kinds of signs that children can already identify. These can be noted by the teacher on a poster called Signs in Our World. The children might then consider if they could do a project all about signs in their world. Are there enough examples of signs around them? What could they do to teach other children about signs? What kinds of signs do they see every day? What is the purpose of signs?

The children should have a lot to say about their experience and knowledge of signs to date. When they have finished sharing their thoughts on this topic, the teacher might propose an excursion into the school neighborhood to note all the signs they can see. She should ask the students to predict what they will see and ask them how they will go about noting these signs. Through drawing and invented spelling, with additional help from the teacher, teaching assistants, and parent volunteers, kindergarten children on such an expedition are capable of identifying and noting many types of signs. Children could decide when they would schedule their excursion. The teacher could look up the weather forecast for that day and they could decide together what they would need to wear to be prepared for an outdoor field trip. As well, they will have to decide what note-taking materials they would need to get all of the important details down.

On a typical excursion in a neighborhood, children will see stop signs, traffic lights, the sign for their school, parking signs, cross-walk signs (and possibly the stop sign that the crossing guard carries), plus directional signs that may simply use arrows but no words. If your school is located in an urban center, there should also be signs for neighborhood shops (shoe repair, dry cleaners, book stores, convenience stores) and restaurants (cafés, fast food places, and pizza shops). If the school is part of a bedroom community suburb, a slow trip in a school bus might be an option for a wider look at signs. No matter what kinds of shops happen to be identified, all will have open and closed signs, push and pull signs, and other common elements such as "Sale" and "New." The children should note all that they can identify with the help of the adult supervisors. A running record of sign sightings could also be made with a digital camera or video.

Back in the classroom, the field trip research can be transcribed by the teacher into a new web in which the children can decide which signs go with which – traffic signs, signs on shops, direction signs, or "what to do" signs. The categories will depend on the children. When they have exhausted all their categories, it might be time to look at the photos or movie of the excursion to check for understanding, possible new categories, or signs that they had forgotten.

 ## Investigation

The investigation stage is now well under way. The children will have a good understanding of traffic signs and commercial signs in their world. At this stage children may be ready to consider other reasons for creating signs. The librarian might read a selection of stories about danger or warnings. Signs already studied in some detail, such as "Stop" or "Do Not Enter" can be posted on the library door, along with other warning signs such as "Danger!" or "Slow!" or "Beware." These signs could have an image of a dangerous creature on them such as an alligator, ferocious dog, bear, or bull. This would depend on the stories that are chosen and the experience of the children (young students in Florida would understand an alligator image immediately, while their counterparts in Alaska might recognize the outline of a polar bear on the loose).

As the children enter the library, the librarian can point out the signs on the door and ask them what they could mean. It won't take them long to make the connection if the librarian is also wearing a construction paper hat with a long green snout with big white triangular teeth adorning the edge! An accompanying puppet can also do the trick. The children will be primed to enjoy a reading of fun and not-too-scary stories about encounters with dangerous animals. A few good examples would be *There's an Alligator Under My Bed* by Mercer Mayer or *The Gruffalo* by Julia Donaldson. An entertaining way to conclude this introductory reading related to signs is to have the teacher enter the library afraid about what she is likely to encounter there.

The children are now ready for nonfiction. And thankfully, there are plenty of excellent choices currently on the market about this topic. Easy informational books for emergent readers such as the "Welcome Books" series on signs are perfect for shared reading between students in the classroom or library, even if they are only reading the pictures and one or two words. These books feature modern children of their age going about daily tasks with parents at the store, the park, the pool, the airport, at school, and on the road, each time noting the signs they see along the way. The teacher or librarian can take note of what they are discussing about these signs. Any new ideas about signs emerging from this shared reading activity should be incorporated into future work on signs.

As children are read more information books about signs, ideas may begin to form about their final project. What signs would they like to use in their final product? What form will that product take? The children might decide to make a town full of signs. This is an idea that may not fit into the dramatic play corner of the classroom. Perhaps an area of the school or playground (depending on the time of year and the weather conditions) can be commandeered for a large installation project. The children might want to create signs and place them around the village or town square. This would then serve as an interactive training ground for other students to practice obeying signs. The video or photo diary of their previous excursion might serve as a model here.

▶ End Product

The children might want to construct a roadway on part of their playground with traffic signs along the way. This could be a temporary design made entirely by the students or a student-designed plan that is then painted as a permanent feature of the playground. In this case, a toy road set that a child has at home might serve as a model, along with the advice of the painter hired to realize their scheme. Their choice might be to decorate their classroom door as the librarian did with signs from a particular story. Whatever the end product, opportunities for content area connections with shapes, colors, words, and categories abound, along with the social skills of collaborative decision-making and division of tasks to achieve a common goal.

 ## Integrating Standards

As usual, language and literacy standards are in evidence throughout this project. Distinguishing real (a visit to the airport) from imaginary (a visit from a gruffalo), using pictures or symbols to identify a concept, recognizing that print corresponds to spoken words, making predictions from pictures, and many other standards are met during this project. The children have engaged with a wide variety of symbols and words in their local environment that support social studies indicators as well. By exploring signs around their town they are learning about their community as well. Health and safety is an important part of this project as well, since the children are learning about how signs help prevent accidents and keep us safe.

Mathematics indicators related to geometry feature prominently in this project. As children take notes about the signs they see they have begun to practice drawing different shapes. This is a task that they will repeat over and over throughout this project. The project approach encourages this sort of repeated practice because it helps children to improve their ability to represent what they have observed. Sorting and classifying activities are present as well, as children discuss the different purposes of signs, shapes of signs, colors of signs, or location of signs. The possibilities are endless. As children note their observations through pictures or with the help of an adult, ask questions about objects, and use their senses, they are achieving standards related to scientific development as well.

 ## Resources for "Signs All Around Us"

Information Books:

Alphabeep: A Zipping, Zooming ABC by Debora Pearson, illustrated by Edward Miller (Holiday House, 2003)

City Signs by Brenda Parkes (Newbridge Educational Pub., 2000)

City Signs by Zoran Milich (Kids Can Press, 2002)

Directions by Henry Arthur Pluckrose, illustrated by Chris Fairclough (Watts, 1992)

Green Means Go by Susan Ring (Yellow Umbrella Books, 2006)

I Read Signs by Tana Hoban (Harcourt, 1983)

I Read Symbols by Tana Hoban (Mulberry Books, 1983)

I See a Sign by Lars Klove (Simon & Schuster Books for Young Readers, 1996)

Red Light, Green Light by Anastasia Suen, illustrated by Ken Wilson-Max (Harcourt, 2005)

Red, Yellow, Green . . . What Do Signs Mean? by Joan Holub (Scholastic, 1998)

Road Signs (Children's Television Network, 2000)

Road Signs: A Harey Race with a Tortoise (An Aesop Fable Adapted) by Margery Cuyler, illustrated by Steve Haskamp (Winslow Press, 2000)

Signs by David Bauer (Yellow Umbrella Books, 2006)

Signs by Diane-Elizabeth Napler (Rainbow Images, 2000)

Signs by Fay Robinson, photographs by Rich Frishman (The Wright Group, 1999)

Signs by Julie Ellis, illustrated by Michael Curtain (Sundance, 2002)

Signs by Susan Canizares, illustrated by Pamela Chanko (Scholastic, 1999)

Signs by Virginia King, illustrated by Kim Roberts (Rigby, 1997)

Signs at School by Mary Hill (Children's Press, 2003)

Signs at the Airport by Mary Hill (Children's Press, 2003)

Signs at the Park by Mary Hill (Children's Press, 2003)

Signs at the Pool by Mary Hill (Children's Press, 2003)

Signs at the Store by Mary Hill (Children's Press, 2003)

Signs Everywhere by Peter Sloan and Sheryl Sloan (Sundance, 1998)

Signs in Our World (DK Publishing, 2006)

Signs on the Road by Mary Hill (Children's Press, 2003)

Signs on the Way by Marvin Buckley (National Geographic, 2001)

Stop! Go! by Lillian Cohen, illustrated by Michele Dorenkamp (Troll 2002)

The Stop Sign by Nancy Parent, illustrated by Adam Devaney (Paradise Press, 2000)

The Traffic Light by Nancy Parent, illustrated by Adam Devaney (Paradise Press, 2000)

The Yield Sign by Nancy Parent, illustrated by Adam Devaney (Paradise Press, 2000)

This Means Stop by Myka-Lynne Sokoloff, illustrated by Larry Paulsen (Scott Foresman/Addison-Wesley, 2002)

Stories and Narratives:

Don't Ever Cross That Road!: An Armadillo Story by Conrad J. Storad, illustrated by Nathaniel P. Jensen (RGU Group, 2003)

Policeman Lou and Policewoman Sue by Lisa Desimini (Blue Sky Press, 2003)

Rush Hour by Christine Loomis, illustrated by Mari Takabayashi (Houghton Mifflin, 1996)

School Bus by Donald Crews (Greenwillow Books, 1984)

Where's Al by Byron Barton (Clarion, 1972)

Video:

Getting to School Safely [videorecording] by Ernie Geefay and Cathy Geefay (100% Educational Videos, 1998, 15 min.)

PROJECT TWO: *It's Autumn*

 Relevance

Seasonal projects are popular with preschool children because they incorporate outdoor observation and exploration with cultural activities and celebrations. Thus, they are relevant as an in-depth project idea. Autumn is a time of stunning change in the color of leaves, the harvest of fruits and vegetables, and in temperature and weather patterns. This is especially so in the New England states and eastern Canada, but all regions have particular changes that can be observed. A project about autumn will necessarily involve both scientific observations and research into the important seasonal celebrations of Halloween and Thanksgiving.

 Discussion

An exploration of autumn can begin with the official first day (Autumn Equinox) or at the first physical signs of change. Either way, children have already had enough direct experience of autumnal sights and activities to join in a discussion of what is to come. Discussion is likely to include the changes to their physical environment in autumn, the special foods and outings associated with the season, plus the particulars of Halloween and Thanksgiving Day. Note-taking in the class can be helped along by stories and nonfiction books read in the library.

 Investigation

As the investigation about autumn develops, children may decide to organize their notes under different headings. These will vary depending on weather where the children live. Northern states and provinces will have different phenomena to observe than in the South. Children in or near rural areas will be more aware of what happens during harvest time. Children may eat different foods for Thanksgiving or may celebrate other festivals as well, such as Days of the Dead or religious holidays.

 End Product

Whatever their observations or cultural background, there are many stories and information books available to enrich their investigation. In fact, they may inspire children to produce their own books about autumn in their part of the world. Children in kindergarten enjoy representational drawing and many can copy particular words. A collective book about some aspect of autumn is doable at this age. Small groups might decide to focus on a cultural, geographical, or scientific book about autumn. It's up to them. As long as they have had enough time for direct observation of nature, plus explanations from books and local experts, they are ready to express what they have learned through drawings and words.

Resources for "It's Autumn"

Informative Stories:

Alligator Arrived with Apples: A Potluck Alphabet Feast by Crescent Dragonwagon, illustrated by Jose Aruego & Ariane Dewey (Aladdin Paperbacks, 1987)

Apples and Pumpkins by Anne Rockwell, illustrated by Lizzy Rockwell (Aladdin Paperbacks, 1989)

Boo! It's Halloween by Wendy Watson (Clarion, 1992)

Clifford's First Autumn by Norman Bridwell (Scholastic, 1997)

Every Autumn Comes the Bear by Jim Arnosky (Putnam & Grosset Group, 1993)

Fall Is Not Easy by Marty Kelley (Zino Press Children's Books, 1998)

Fall Leaves by Mary Packard, illustrated by Dana Regan (Scholastic, 1999)

Fall Leaves Fall! by Zoe Hall, illustrated by Shari Halpern (Scholastic, 2000)

Fat Chance Thanksgiving by Patricia Lakin, illustrated by Stacey Schuett (Albert Whitman, 2001)

Four Friends in Autumn by Tomie dePaola (Simon & Schuster Books for Young Readers, 2004)

Hello, Harvest Moon by Ralph Fletcher, illustrated by Kate Kiesler (Clarion Books, 2003)

How Many Days to America?: A Thanksgiving Story by Eve Bunting, illustrated by Beth Peck (Clarion Books, 1988)

I Am the Turkey by Michele Sobel Spirn, illustrated by Joy Allen (HarperCollins, 2004)

I Know It's Autumn by Eileen Spinelli, illustrated by Nancy Hayashi (HarperCollins, 2004)

In November by Cynthia Rylant, illustrated by Jill Kastner (Harcourt, 2000)

In the Woods: Who's Been Here? by Lindsay Barrett George (Greenwillow Books, 1995)

It's Fall! by Linda Glaser, illustrated by Susan Swan (Millbrook Press, 2001)

It's Pumpkin Time! by Zoe Hall, illustrated by Shari Halpern (Blue Sky Press, 1994)

Lionel in the Fall by Stephen Krensky, illustrated by Susanna Natti (Puffin Books, 1987)

Moon Glowing by Elizabeth Partridge, illustrated by Joan Paley (Dutton Children's Books, 2002)

Nursery Crimes by Arthur Geisert (Houghton Mifflin, 2001)

Possum's Harvest Moon by Anne Hunter (Houghton Mifflin, 1996)

Setting the Turkeys Free by W. Nikola-Lisa, illustrated by Ken Wilson-Max (Hyperion Books for Children, 2004)

Thanksgiving Day by Anne Rockwell, illustrated by Lizzy Rockwell (HarperCollins, 1999)

Thanksgiving Is Here! by Diane Goode (HarperCollins, 2003)

The Fierce Yellow Pumpkin by Margaret Wise Brown, illustrated by Richard Egielski (HarperCollins, 2003)

The Memory Cupboard: A Thanksgiving Story by Charlotte Herman, illustrated by Ben F. Stahl (Albert Whitman, 2003)

The Perfect Thanksgiving by Eileen Spinelli, illustrated By Joann Adinolfi (Henry Holt, 2003)

The Perfectly Horrible Halloween by Nancy Poydar (Holiday House, 2001)

The Stranger by Chris Van Allsburg (Houghton Mifflin, 1986)

The Thanksgiving Beast Feast by Karen Gray Ruelle (Holiday House, 1999)

The Thanksgiving Door by Debby Atwell (Houghton Mifflin, 2003)

The Ugly Pumpkin by Dave Horowitz (G.P. Putnam's Sons, 2005)

This Is the Turkey by Abby Levine, illustrated by Paige Billin-Frye (Albert Whitman, 2000)

When Autumn Falls by Kelli Nidey, illustrated by Susan Swan (Albert Whitman, 2004)

Information Books:

A to Z of Autumn by Tracy Nelson Maurer (Rourke Pub., 2003)

An Apple Festival: Orchards in Autumn by Lisa Gabbert (PowerKids Press, 1999)

Animals in the Fall by Gail Saunders-Smith (Pebble Books, 1998)

Autumn by Gail Saunders-Smith (Pebble Books, 1998)

Autumn by Terri Degezelle (Bridgestone Books, 2003)

Autumn Leaves by Gail Saunders-Smith (Pebble Books, 1998)

Autumn: Signs of the Season around North America by Mary Pat Finnegan, illustrated by Jeremy Schultz (Picture Window Books, 2003)

Fall by Cynthia Klingel and Robert B. Noyed (Child's World, 2001)

Fall by Darlene Stille (Compass Point Books, 2001)

Fall by Jill Kalz (Creative Education, 2006)

Fall by Moira Butterfield, illustrated by Helen James (Smart Apple Media, 2006)

Fall by Tanya Thayer (Lerner, 2002)

Fall by Vic Parker (Raintree, 2005)

Fall Leaves Change Colors by Kathleen Weidner Zoehfeld (Scholastic Reference, 2001)

Giving Thanks: A Native American Good Morning Message by Chief Jake Swamp, illustrated by Erwin Printup, Jr. (Lee & Low, 1995)

Halloween Is – by Gail Gibbons (Holiday House, 2002)

How Do You Know It's Fall? by Allan Fowler (Children's Press, 1992)

Now It's Fall by Lois Lenski [colorized version, 2000] (Random House, 1948)

Pablo Remembers: The Fiesta of the Days of the Dead by George Ancona (Lothrop, Lee & Shepard Books, 1993)

Thank You, Sarah: The Woman Who Saved Thanksgiving by Laurie Halse Anderson, illustrated by Matt Faulkner (Simon & Schuster Books for Young Readers, 2002)

Thanksgiving by Alice K. Flanagan, illustrated by Kathie Kelleher (Compass Point Books, 2002)

Thanksgiving Is – by Gail Gibbons (Holiday House, 2004)

This First Thanksgiving Day: A Counting Story by Laura Krauss Melmed, illustrated by Mark Buehner (HarperCollins, 2001)

What Happens In Fall? by Sara L. Latta (Enslow Publishers, 2006)

When Autumn Comes by Robert Maass (Henry Holt, 1990)

Why Do Leaves Change Color? by Betsy Maestro, illustrated by Loretta Krupinski (HarperCollins, 1994)

Video:

Fall Brings Changes [videorecording] text and music by Jim Burroughs (A Churchill Film, 1991, 15 min.)

Giving Thanks: A Native American Good Morning Message [videorecording] by Daniel Ivanick (Weston Woods, Westport, Conn., 1997, 7 min.)

Thanksgiving Day [videorecording] by Gail Gibbons (Live Oak Media, 1993, 6 min.)

Songs and Poems:

Angels Ride Bikes and Other Fall Poems: Poems = Los Angeles Andan en Bicicleta y Otros Poemas de Otono: Poemas by Francisco X. Alarcon, illustrated by Maya Christina Gonzalez (Children's Book Press/Libros Para Ninos, 1999)

Celebrations by Myra Cohn Livingston, illustrated by Leonard Everett Fisher (Holiday House, 1985)

It's Thanksgiving by Jack Prelutsky, illustrated by Marylin Hafner (Greenwillow Books, 1982)

John Mccutcheon's Four Seasons: Autumnsongs [sound recording] (Rounder Kids, 1995)

Over the River and through the Wood by Lydia Maria Child, illustrated by David Catrow (Henry Holt, 1999)

Piggyback Songs [sound recording] [includes "Autumn Leaves"] (Kimbo Educational, 1995)

Pumpkin Eye by Denise Fleming (Henry Holt, 2001)

Pumpkin Jack by Will Hubbell (Albert Whitman, 2000)

Scary, Scary Halloween by Eve Bunting, illustrated by Jan Brett (Clarion Books, 1986)

Thanksgiving Day at Our House: Thanksgiving Poems for the Very Young by Nancy White Carlstrom, illustrated by R.W. Alley (Aladdin Paperbacks, 1999)

The Witch Casts a Spell by Suzanne Williams, illustrated by Barbara Olsen (Dial Books for Young Readers, 2002)

PROJECT THREE: *All Day Long*

 Relevance

Children in kindergarten are not quite ready to learn about an abstract concept like time, but they are aware of the way activities change throughout the day and are now quite used to following a schedule of classes at school. Preschool children appreciate regularity and predictability in their lives. If they have been in preschool from the age of three they are already experts on the way a day is organized. An inquiry into the pattern of a typical day is something they know from first-hand experience and thus qualifies as a relevant and engaging project idea.

 Discussion

Many songs and stories recount the feelings, sights, and sounds that greet us upon waking up. From the lovely story of a boy with an early paper route (*Paperboy*) to the joyful *Morning Song* to the silly *Bedhead*, stories abound about morning and daytime routines that children can relate to. Beginning a project with songs and stories will help to bring ideas and comments to this preliminary discussion stage of the project. Once children have begun to get their ideas down on paper with the help of the teacher, they are ready to decide upon a feasible project approach to the topic "All Day Long." Groups of children might decide to describe each day of the week in the form of a photo journal, with a group for Monday through Friday. With the help of a digital camera at school and with parents, morning routines, transportation to school, and typical activities can be documented.

 Investigation

Dialogic readings of stories and nonfiction will give the children ideas about what they might include in their investigation. Parents might come in as guest speakers to talk about all of the logistical problems there are to organizing a day, such as watching the time and planning for heavy traffic. Patterns should soon become apparent to the children and commonalities are sure to receive special attention. Do many children travel by bus? Do parents carpool? Do they have babysitters or stay with grandparents after school? Do they eat supper at the same time? Do they play certain games after school? What routines, such as brushing their teeth, saying prayers, having a bedtime story, or taking a bath make up their day? Whatever they finally focus on, an in-depth exploration of patterns of daily life will help them appreciate the more abstract ideas of time passing and the importance of organization in our lives.

 End Product

The documentation provided by the digital camera makes it easy to put together a chronological presentation such as a timeline. Other options children might consider would be to arrange the photographs with captions on a poster or in the form of a book or brochure.

 ## Resources for "All Day Long"

Stories:

And if the Moon Could Talk by Kate Banks, illustrated by Georg Hallensleben (Frances Foster Books, 1998)

Bedhead by Margie Palatini, illustrated by Jack E. Davis (Simon & Schuster Books for Young Readers, 2000)

Breakfast for Jack by Pat Schories (Front Street, 2004)

Bunny Day: Telling Time from Breakfast to Bedtime by Rick Walton, illustrated by Paige Miglio (HarperCollins, 2002)

Buzz by Janet S. Wong, illustrated by Margaret Chodos-Irvine (Harcourt, 2000)

Chugga-Chugga Choo-Choo by Kevin Lewis, illustrated by Daniel Kirk (Hyperion Books for Children, 1999)

Cluck O'Clock by Kes Gray, illustrated by Mary Mcquillan (Holiday House, 2003)

Dad and Me in the Morning by Patricia Lakin, illustrated by Robert Steele (Albert Whitman, 1994)

Farm Morning by David Mcphail (Harcourt Brace Jovanovich, 1985)

Giggle-Wiggle Wake-Up! by Nancy White Carlstrom, illustrated by Melissa Sweet (Knopf, 2003)

Good Day, Good Night by Marilyn Singer, illustrated by Ponder Geombel (Marshall Cavendish, 1998)

Good Morning Sam by Marie-Louise Gay (Douglas & Mcintyre, 2003)

Good Morning, Garden by Barbara Brenner, illustrated by Denise Ortakales (Northword Press, 2004)

Jesse Bear, What Will You Wear? by Nancy White Carlstrom, illustrated by Bruce Degen (Simon & Schuster Books for Young Readers, Collier Macmillan, 1986)

Ji Doo Tl'ee' = Day and Night by Nedra Emery, illustrated by Verna Clinton (Salina Bookshelf, 1996)

Just Another Morning by Linda Ashman, illustrated by Claudio Munoz (HarperCollins, 2004)

Kitten's First Full Moon by Kevin Henkes (Greenwillow Books, 2004)

Mei-Mei Loves the Morning by Margaret Tsubakiyama, illustrated by Cornelius Van Wright and Ying-Hwa Hu (Albert Whitman, 1999)

Millie Wants to Play! by Janet Pedersen (Candlewick Press, 2004)

Morning Song by Mary McKenna Siddals, illustrated by Elizabeth Sayles (Henry Holt, 2001)

Morning, Noon, and Night by Jean Craighead George, illustrated by Wendell Minor (HarperCollins, 1999)

Rise and Shine by Raffi, Bonnie Simpson, and Bert Simpson, illustrated by Eugenie Fernandes (Crown Publishers, 1996)

Rush Hour by Christine Loomis, illustrated by Mari Takabayashi (Houghton Mifflin, 1996)

Shhhh by Kevin Henkes (Greenwillow Books, 1989)

Sunshine by Jan Ormerod (Frances Lincoln's Children's Books, 1981)

Tell Me What It's Like to Be Big by Joyce Dunbar, illustrated by Debi Gliori (Harcourt, 2001)

Telling Time with Big Mama Cat by Dan Harper, illustrated by Barry Moser and Cara Moser (Harcourt Brace, 1998)

The Elves and the Shoemaker retold from the Brothers Grimm by Jim Lamarche (Chronicle Books, 2003)

The Milkman by Carol Foskett Cordsen, illustrated by Douglas B. Jones (Dutton Children's Books, 2005)

The Paperboy by Dav Pilkey (Orchard Books, 1996)

The Stars Are Waiting by Marjorie Dennis Murray, illustrated by Jacqueline Rogers (Marshall Cavendish, 1998)

Wake Up, Me! by Marni McGee, illustrated by Sam Williams (Simon & Schuster Books for Young Readers, 2002)

Zee by Michel Gay, translation by Marie Mianowski (Clarion Books, 2003)

Poems:

From Daybreak to Good Night: Poems for Children by Carl Sandburg, illustrated by Lynn Smith-Ary (Annick Press, 2001)

Hello Sunshine, Good Night Moonlight by Eleanor Farjeon et al., illustrated by John Wallace (Harry N. Abrams, 2004)

I Like Stars by Margaret Wise Brown, illustrated by Joan Paley (Golden Books, 1998)

Morning, Noon, and Night: Poems to Fill Your Day selected by Sharon Taberski, illustrated by Nancy Doniger (Mondo Publishing, 1996)

The Sound of Day, the Sound of Night by Mary O'Neill, illustrated by Cynthia Jabar (Farrar, Straus and Giroux, 2003)

Wake Up House!: Rooms Full of Poems by Dee Lillegard, illustrated by Don Carter (Dragonfly Books, 2000)

Wake Up, Sleepy Head!: Early Morning Poems by Mandy Ross, illustrated by Dubravka Kolanovic (Child's Play, 2004)

Songs:

American Folksongs for Children by Mike Seeger (Rounder Kids, 1996 [Includes "Oh, Oh the Sunshine," "I Got a Letter This Morning"])

Good Morning Exercises for Kids [sound recording] by Georgiana Stewart [includes "Zippity Doo Dah," "It's a Great Getting Up Morning," "Oh What a Beautiful Morning"] (Kimbo, 1987)

Waltzing with Fireflies [sound recording] by Elizabeth McMahon and Rosie Rhubarb, [includes "Earth Is Still Sleeping," "I Love the Morning"] (Kimbo, 1987)

We Are America's Children [sound recording] by Ella Jenkins [includes "I Woke Up This Morning"] (Smithsonian/Folkways, 1989)

Wee Sing Children's Songs and Fingerplays [sound recording] by Pamela Conn Beall and Susan Hagen Nipp [includes "Good Morning," "Good Night"] (Price Stern Sloan, 2005)

Nonfiction:

A Busy Day by Brian Sargent (Children's Press, 2006)

A Day by Patricia J. Murphy (Capstone Press, 2005)

A Good Night's Sleep by Allan Fowler (Children's Press, 1996)

A Good Night's Sleep by Sharon Gordon (Children's Press, 2002)

Animals Day and Night by Katharine Kenah (McGraw-Hill Children's Pub., 2004)

Bright Lights and Shadowy Shapes by Jennifer Waters (Compass Point Books, 2002)

By Day and By Night by Valérie Guidoux, illustrated by Regis Faller, Olivier Nadel, Philippe Mignon, and Charlotte Roederer (Firefly Books, 2006)

Day and Night by Anita Ganeri (Heinemann Library, 2004)

Day and Night by Henry Pluckrose (Gareth Stevens, 2001)

Day Light, Night Light: Where Light Comes From by Franklyn M. Branley, illustrated by Stacey Schuett (HarperCollins, 1998)

Days of the Week by Jilly Attwood (Raintree, 2005)

First Day at School by Monica Hughes (Raintree, 2004)

Forest Bright, Forest Night; Forest Night, Forest Bright by Jennifer Ward, illustrated by Jamichael Henterly (Dawn, 2005)

Fun with the Sun by Melissa Stewart, illustrated by Jeffrey Scherer (Compass Point Books, 2004)

It's About Time! by Stuart J. Murphy, illustrated by John Speirs (HarperCollins, 2005)

Morning Meals Around the World by Maryellen Gregoire, illustrated by Jeff Yesh (Picture Window Books, 2004)

My Bedtime: A Book About Getting Ready for Bed by Heather Feldman, photographs by Thaddeus Harden (PowerKids Press, 2000)

My Breakfast: A Book About a Great Morning Meal by Heather Feldman, photographs by John Bentham (PowerKids Press, 2000)

My Day by Henry Pluckrose (Gareth Stevens, 2001)

My First Book of Time by Claire Llewellyn (DK Publishing, 1992)

Night and Day by Alvin Granowsky, illustrated by Mary Lonsdale (Copper Beech Books, 2001)

What Can I – Feel? by Sue Barraclough (Raintree, 2005)

What Makes Day and Night by Franklyn M. Branley, illustrated by Arthur Dorros (HarperCollins, 1986)

When Morning Comes by Ron Hirschi, photographs by Thomas D. Mangelsen (Caroline House, 2000)

When Night Comes by Ron Hirschi, photographs by Thomas D. Mangelsen (Caroline House, 2000)

PROJECT FOUR: *School Bus*

 ## Relevance

School bus projects are quite common in schools that use the project approach. The obvious reason is that most schools in North America bus children to school. The bus ride to school is an important feature of each day and one that children are curious about. Because the school bus is part of their everyday experience, this is a relevant topic for kindergarten children to explore.

 ## Investigation

Get children talking about their experience on the school bus and the questions that they might have. It will become clear that there is a lot to learn about this subject and that it is worthy of serious investigation. Ask yourself if you know how many wheels a school bus has. Why are school buses yellow? Why are modern school buses flat in the front? What is the long shift stick for? How fast does the bus go? How many stops does it make? How many children travel by bus? How many bus drivers does the school have? Do some children take regular city buses? How do they pay for the ride?

The school's bus drivers are readily available experts who can be interviewed by the children and who can lead children on a "field trip" that is convenient and safe since it takes place on school property. Children can use small whiteboards or clipboards and paper to take down information in the form of pictures and words. Children can use invented spelling or ask adults to scribe for them as comments and questions arise. Again, a digital camera can be of great help in documenting how things look.

 ## End Product

Typically children choose to make a replica of a school bus as their end product. This is especially appealing since it can be used as an interactive area for dramatic play once it is completed. Though it may be roughly constructed of large boxes and cardboard, information from their hands-on investigation and interviews will provide the bus with accurate details. Children can then guide other adults, such as the principal or visiting parents, around the bus to point out its special features and functions, much as the bus drivers did for them.

 ## Resources for "School Bus"

Stories:

Bones and the Big Yellow Mystery by David A. Adler, illustrated by Barbara
    Johansen Newman (Viking, 2004)

Hello, School Bus! by Marjorie Blain Parker, illustrated by Bob Kolar (Scholastic, 2004)

Max Goes on the Bus by Adria Klein, illustrated by Mernie Gallagher-Cole (Picture Window Books, 2006)

Molly Rides the School Bus by Julie Brillhart (Albert Whitman, 2002)

The Bus for Us by Suzanne Bloom (Boyds Mills Press, 2001)

The Little School Bus by Carol Roth, illustrated by Pamela Paparone (North-South Books, 2002)

The Seals on the Bus by Lenny Hort, illustrated by G. Brian Karas (Henry Holt, 2000)

Information Books:

Be Safe on the Bus by Kathy Smith (PowerKids Press, 2002)

Going By Bus by Susan Ashley (Weekly Reader Early Learning, 2004)

I Spy a School Bus: Riddles by Jean Marzollo, photographs by Walter Wick (Scholastic, 2003)

My School Bus: A Book About School Bus Safety by Heather Feldman, photographs by Donna M. Scholl (PowerKids Press, 2000)

Riding the School Bus with Mrs. Kramer by Alice K. Flanagan, photographs by Christine Osinski (Children's Press, 1998)

Safety on the School Bus by Lucia Raatma (Bridgestone Books, 1999)

School Bus by Donald Crews (Greenwillow Books, 1984)

School Bus Drivers by Melanie Mitchell, photographs by Jim Baron (Lerner, 2005)

School Buses by Dee Ready (Bridgestone Books, 1998)

Taking You Places: A Book About Bus Drivers by Ann Owen, illustrated by Eric Thomas (Picture Window Books, 2004)

Songs:

The Wheels on the Bus edited by Ann Owen, illustrated by Sandra D'Antonio (Picture Window Books, 2003)

Cars, Trucks and Trains [sound recording] by Jane Murphy [includes "School Bus," "Whee! Whee! Wheels!," and "Signs and Signals"] (Kimbo Educational, 1997)

Rise and Shine [sound recording] by Raffi [includes "Wheels on the Bus"] (Shoreline, 1982)

Video:

School Buses [videorecording] by Cynthia Klingel and Robert B. Noyed (Child's World, 2001, 13 min.)

School Bus Safety [videorecording] (100% Educational Video, 1997)

Chapter Six

Research and Inquiry in Grade One

Working With Children in Grade One

Children in grade one now have "considerable verbal ability" (Bredekamp 6). Their language skills are employed in playing games, often ones with fairly complex rules. These experiences help them develop good problem-solving skills.

Six-year-olds are in the middle of what is known as the 5- to 7-year shift, a term first coined by Sheldon White in 1965 (Sameroff and McDonough). As noted in Chapter 2, young children *can* accomplish tasks normally thought to have been a part of this 5- to 7-year-old stage of development. Piaget's strict system of developmental stages has been called into question to some extent as a result of recent research into cognitive stages. Researchers have found that by simplifying tasks and supporting children's efforts, many cognitive abilities thought to be exclusive to 5- to 7-year-olds, such as the ability to speak in complex sentences, can be accomplished by much younger children.

What remains true is that for younger children, achieving these cognitive feats requires the individual attention of an adult. As well, the young child has to be highly motivated by a task that is relevant to him (Sameroff and McDonough). During the 5- to 7-year shift, children are developing a deeper understanding of how the world works. When faced with a phenomenon or problem, they can approach it from many perspectives. An appreciation of the fact that other children may have different opinions or views on a given topic has developed. Children in this age range can offer arguments that provide evidence of reasoning about several aspects of a problem at once. When they classify things they can "consider more than one level at a time in a conceptual hierarchy" and they know "the difference between all and some" (Sameroff and McDonough).

As six-year-olds grow in their ability to read and write, so too does their ability to think in more abstract terms. Children at this age will still vary widely, but some will certainly be very active and eager readers. Some children will prefer certain authors or types of books and they will be able to articulate these preferences. Thus, projects cannot only grow in complexity, but also they can be different for different children, depending on the choices that the children make according to their personal interests. This will require a wider range of resources than in previous years, but they are resources that will continue to be useful as they move beyond their early childhood education.

Informational Strategies in Grade One

As beginning readers and writers, there are many informational strategies that children can use and that teachers and librarians can model. These strategies demonstrate the children's growing independence as readers, writers, and researchers.

- Children are asked to write one sentence captions to accompany their own drawings and photographs.

- In pairs, children explore simple nonfiction texts for answers to student-generated questions.

- In pairs, children use highlighter tape to select the most important or "key" word on each page of an early informational book.

- Children are asked to use both images and text to find answers to questions.

- Children produce representative drawings and label parts of these drawings.

- Children use table of contents (with keywords highlighted with highlighter tape if necessary) to find the part of an informational book that will address their question.

- Children use photographs and captions from more difficult informational books to find answers to questions.

- Children use headings and photographs to scan a page in an information book for possible answers.

- Children read informative stories and nonfiction together from large e-book projections.

- Teachers and librarians scribe note-taking of both questions and answers during discussions, explorations, and research sessions.

- Teachers and librarians post written lists of questions, plans, or procedures during the course of a project.

Projects

PROJECT ONE: *Animal Friends*

 Relevance

Animals are a perennial favorite as a topic for research because it is meaningful and relevant to children. Many children today have pets or have had experience with domestic animals. Even those without pets may still have a preference for a particular kind of pet. Children may sometimes be tempted to tease or hurt a small animal. Some may be fearful of certain animals. This project work will teach children how to treat animals and what can be expected of them. Stories about animal friends are especially important in raising awareness and sympathy for animals.

 Discussion

Discussion of animals often comes up in a grade one classroom. Many stories for children feature animals and these usually spark comments about the animals that the children have at home. Thus, a good way to test the waters for this project idea is simply to read a few good stories about animals that will stimulate a lot of commentary and questions from the children. In this way, the discussion is initiated by the children themselves.

Since cats and dogs are the most popular pets in the United States, it is important to have lots of examples of stories that feature feline and canine characters in your school library. These books are sure to encourage a good discussion about pets. One recent title that grade one students find intriguing is *The Cat Who Walked Across France* by Kate Banks. With evocative paintings of well-known French landmarks that some of the children might recognize, this story tells of an "incredible journey" type of tale as a cat seeks to find his old home. A similar – and true – story is *Go Home: The True Story of James the Cat* by Libby Phillips Meggs. This endearing tale describes the difficult life of a stray cat until he is finally taken in by a family. *Nobody's Nosier Than a Cat* by Susan Campbell Bartoletti has lots to teach children about the habits of real-life cats. In *Pinky and Rex and the Just-Right Pet* by James Howe, a little boy learns to love a kitten.

An early chapter book that makes a funny read-aloud is *Dragon's Fat Cat* by Dav Pilkey. Dragon's bungling attempts to take care of his new cat is a good lesson in what a cat really needs to be healthy and happy. Dav Pilkey has many funny books about pets: *Hally Tosis*, *Kat Kong*, and *Dogzilla* are big hits with students of this age, as is the more realistic picture book, *The Paperboy,* about the close relationship between a boy and his dog. A similar book about a boy and his dog is *My Dog Talks* by Gail Herman. Other good stories featuring dogs are *Any Kind of Dog* by Lynn Reiser, *Arthur's New Puppy* by Marc Brown, and *My Dog's the Best* by Stephanie Calmenson.

Aside from cats and dogs, the resources listed for this project include stories about frogs, mice, rats, birds, and even boa constrictors. Many other animal friends are featured in the true tales of animal friends by the charming Dick King-Smith. All of these stories, imaginary or true, make great read-alouds for library or classroom sessions. Any comments that are made during library sessions can be noted for use back in the classroom.

 ## Investigation

Once the children are talking about animal friends, the investigation is sure to take off. In the classroom, the teacher can ask children to tell her about animals that make good pets. This usually sets off some lively debates among the children as some weirder examples of potential pets are raised. Children should be encouraged to talk about their own pets and their experiences with them. Often this kind of sharing will lead to stories about the death of pets, even with very young children. Two good books to have on hand that treat this subject well are *Desser, the Best Ever Cat* by Maggie Smith and *The Old Dog* by Charlotte Zolotow. All of this discussion will become part of the classroom's web diagram about the topic "Animal Friends."

Before children are asked about their project ideas it is useful to have them think about just how many kinds of pets there are. This will ensure that all of the children don't end up wanting to do just dogs and cats. An entertaining and informative video on this topic is *Animal Pets* from Dorling Kindersley. The related topic of how we care for animals can give them more focus when considering their questions about animals. Another video, *Growing Up Well: Paws, Claws, Feathers & Fins: A Kid's Video Guide to Pets* covers this topic well.

▶ End Product

Now the students are ready to make decisions about what kind of end product they will produce to help teach people about pets. A likely outcome is a book or video about pet care. Either way, the final outcome will involve a presentation, either live or taped, about how to care for a certain type of animal. At this stage, it is not necessary for the children to make a firm decision about what kind of animal they will research. The teacher can let them know that they will see many kinds of animals described in books at the library. She can even present the children with a listing from the librarian of animals that the library resources cover well enough to complete a project.

At this point the children must decide with whom they will work and what kinds of questions their book or video presentations will cover. To make the evaluation process fair, the class must agree on which questions their final product will address. Because their writing skills are not well developed, it is best to keep the answers simple. Many questions about pets can be answered by a list of words. For example, children might want to talk about what their pet eats. The answer is a list of at least five different foods. This then becomes part of the rubric for judging the book or video.

Other questions that can be answered by word lists are: Our pet likes to: _____ (jump, play, fetch, roll over, etc.); Our pet needs: _____ (a warm bed, a litter box, toys, a collar, etc.); Our pet is: _____ (soft, small, furry, curious, etc.); You should never: _____ (pull its tail, tease it, scare it, etc.) Children will often want to include pictures of their own animals if they have pets at home. This makes a nice conclusion to a book or video.

Once the statements have all been written out as a model for the children to follow, the teacher may decide it is time to make a presentation of a book or a video to the class. This will help children to complete their evaluative guidelines for what the final product should look like and include. Children may want to include a picture on each page of the book. Objects used in the care and feeding of pets can be brought to school by the children. These items are especially useful for a video presentation. All of the elements that are necessary to the final product, guidelines about their appearance, and notes about making a good presentation should be clearly articulated and posted in the classroom.

Children are now ready to research their chosen animals at the library. Each group should have five research sheets, with each statement begun at the top of the page: A cat eats _____, A cat likes to _____, A cat needs _____, A cat is _____, and You should never _____. If the children want to include pictures of their own pets, a sixth page can be headed "Our Pets." Pictures can be pasted in and names of pets written below each picture. Finally, the librarian should provide the students with a worksheet with the statement: "For this book (or video) I used these titles for my research." Some words may have already been noted based on read-alouds and videos about pets. If so, the titles of these sources should be written on this title sheet right away. The teacher can now add another requirement to the evaluation rubric: "The book or video concludes with a list of the titles of materials that we have used during our research."

Children will search informational stories, nonfiction texts, encyclopedias, and their online database. These resources are listed at the end of this chapter. Because students will be new to using so many resources in different formats, it is important that they are giving plenty of scaffolding by both the teacher and librarian during their library sessions.

First of all, the children will need help locating information. At this stage in their experience with library research, it is best to pre-select the resources and concentrate on helping children to find information within sources than to try to instill Dewey designations. Children will have a lot to master just learning how to find information using the index and table of contents, to scan for information, and to interpret information from photos and diagrams. Some of the resources will be too difficult for some students, so they will need to be helped to seek out small snippets of information from picture captions or to scan for words in bold.

The students will not be able to complete their research in one session, so further bookings into the library will have to be made as their progress is monitored. In the meantime, to sustain interest in the project and to continue to develop their knowledge of pets, experts can be brought in to answer questions that their first look at secondary information sources may have raised. A question period with a veterinarian, pet shop owner, or obedience school trainer might help. Parents could be asked to volunteer to bring pets from home, within the school's regulations about animals in the classrooms. Firsthand experience is especially important if a group chooses an unusual animal, such as a chinchilla or gray parrot, animals that most of the children may never have actually seen before.

As their research sheets are filled with lists of answers, the teacher and librarian need to monitor that the children are keeping the evaluation rubrics in mind. Have the children listed five terms for each question? Have they drawn at least one picture for each page in their book? Have they decided who will bring in objects to use during their presentations? Have they written down the titles of all the resources they have used?

The teacher and librarian can work together to coach the children about their final presentation. Once the research sheets are ready, they can be retyped or rewritten if the children desire, the sheets can go into a booklet form as is, or the pictures and words can be cut and pasted onto heavier weight sheets to form a sturdier booklet suitable for coil binding. The children might prefer to staple the booklet together or punch holes and tie them with ribbons. Of course, they will need to design a cover for the booklet. If the children haven't already suggested this as part of their evaluation guidelines, the librarian should prompt them to compare the books that they are using for research to the booklet that they are writing. Children will soon realize that the booklet with need a specially designed front and back cover. If the children are doing a video, they will need to practice what they will say based on their research sheets and the extra objects that they have brought in to present. If the children are writing a booklet, they need to practice reading parts of their booklet before an adult audience in order to improve their presentation skills.

The students may decide to present to their classmates first, then to present to a larger audience of parents or other students afterwards. Whatever they choose to do, the teacher and librarian should be there to help them successfully achieve all the goals that they have set.

 ## Integrating Standards

This project clearly meets standards related to scientific development. Taking an example of grade one standards from Arizona, all four general science concepts are addressed in "Animal Friends:" the children are making observations, asking questions, and proposing hypotheses; the children are planning and conducting investigations of pets that are brought into the classroom and recording what they observe; the children organize data both from direct observation and reading of informational books; and the children complete the project by communicating the results of their investigations. In addition, standards that relate specifically to life science are met as well. Basic structures of various animals are observed and their function is noted. Children learn about the varying life cycles of common pets. They learn about the needs of different organisms.

But this project is not just about science. The many stories that they have read about pets have also taught them about other cultures. Important dispositions such as curiosity are addressed. Social and emotional standards related to self-regulation and working with others are met. Many literacy indicators related to all areas of the standards are present: reading, writing, listening, speaking, viewing, and presenting.

 ## Resources for "Animal Friends"

Stories:

Any Kind of Dog by Lynn Reiser (Mulberry, 1994)

Arthur's New Puppy by Marc Brown (Little, Brown, 1993)

Dog Breath! Horrible Trouble with Hally Tosis by Dav Pilkey (Blue Sky Press, 1994)

Dogzilla by Dav Pilkey (Harcourt Children's Books, 1993)

Ginger by Charlotte Voake (Candlewick, 1997)

Kat Kong by Dav Pilkey (Harcourt Children's Books, 1993)

I Took My Frog to the Library by Eric A. Kimmel (Puffin Books, 1992)

I.Q. Goes to the Library by Mary Ann Fraser (Walker, 2003)

Junie B. Jones Smells Something Fishy by Barbara Park, illustrated by Denise Brunkus (Random House, 1998)

Mole and the Baby Bird by Marjorie Newman, illustrated by Patrick Benson (Bloomsbury Children's Books, 2002)

Mouse Views: What the Class Pet Saw by Bruce McMillan (Holiday House, 1993)

My Dog Talks by Gail Herman, illustrated by Ron Fritz (Scholastic, 1995)

My Dog's the Best by Stephanie Calmenson, illustrated by Marcy Dunn Ramsey (Scholastic, 1997)

Pinky and Rex and the Just-Right Pet by James Howe, illustrated by Melissa Sweet (Atheneum Books for Young Readers, 2001)

That Pesky Rat by Lauren Child (Candlewick Press, 2002)

The Cat Who Walked Across France by Kate Banks, illustrated by Georg Hallensleben (Frances Foster Books, 2003)

The Day Jimmy's Boa Ate the Wash by Trinka Hakes Noble, illustrated by Steven Kellogg (Dial Press, 1980)

The Great Pet Sale by Mick Inkpen (Orchard Books, 1998)

The Paperboy by Dav Pilkey (Orchard Books, 1996)

Too Much Trouble for Grandpa by Rob Lewis (Mondo, 1998)

Willie's Wonderful Pet by Mel Cebulash, illustrated by George Ford (Scholastic, 1993)

Informative Stories:

Desser, the Best Ever Cat by Maggie Smith (Knopf Books for Young Readers, 2001)

Dick King-Smith's Animal Friends: Thirty-One True Life Stories by Dick King-Smith, illustrated by Anita Jeram (Candlewick Press, 1996)

Dragon's Fat Cat by Dav Pilkey (Orchard Books, 1995)

Go Home: The True Story of James the Cat by Libby Phillips Meggs (Albert Whitman, 2000)

Nobody's Nosier Than a Cat by Susan Campbell Bartoletti, illustrated by Beppe Giacobbe (Hyperion Books for Children, 2003)

The Best Pet Yet by Louise Vitellaro Tidd, photographs by Dorothy Handelman (Millbrook Press, 1998)

The Old Dog by Charlotte Zolotow, illustrated by James Ransome (HarperCollins, 1995)

Nonfiction Picture Books:

Calico's Cousins: Cats from Around the World by Phyllis Limbacher Tildes (Charlesbridge, 1999)

The True-or-False Book of Cats by Patricia Lauber, illustrated by Rosalyn Schanzer (HarperCollins, 1998)

The True-or-False Book of Dogs by Patricia Lauber, illustrated by Rosalyn Schanzer (HarperCollins, 2003)

Videos:

Animal Pets (DK Vision, 1998, 30 min.)

Growing Up Well: Paws, Claws, Feathers & Fins: A Kid's Video Guide to Pets (Inspired Corporation, 1993, DVD release 2002, 28 min.)

Information Books for Research:

Animal Hospital by Judith Walker-Hodge (DK Publishing, 1999)

Animals by Steve Pollock, photographs by Paul Bricknell and Simon Pugh, illustrations by Salvatore Tomaselli (BBC, 1995)

Animals as Friends by Sally Morgan (Franklin Watts, 1999)

Birds by Ann Larkin Hansen (ABDO & Daughters, 1997)

Cats by Ann Larkin Hansen (ABDO & Daughters, 1997)

Cats by Michaela Miller (Heinemann Interactive Library, 1998)

Chinchillas by Tom Handford (Heinemann Library, 2003)

Dogs by Ann Larkin Hansen (ABDO & Daughters, 1997)

Dogs by Michaela Miller (Heinemann Interactive Library, 1998)

Ferrets by June McNicholas (Heinemann Library, 2003)

Geckos by Sonia Hernandez-Divers (Heinemann Library, 2003)

Goldfish by Michaela Miller (Heinemann Interactive Library, 1998)

Guinea Pigs by Michaela Miller (Heinemann Interactive Library, 1998)

Hamster by Michaela Miller (Heinemann Interactive Library, 1998)

Hamsters and Gerbils by Ann Larkin Hansen (ABDO & Daughters, 1997)

How to Look After Your Pet Kitten: A Practical Guide to Caring for Your Kitten by Mark Evans (DK Publishing, 1992)

It Could Still Be a Cat by Allan Fowler (Children's Press, 1993)

Kitten Care by Kim Dennis-Bryan (DK Publishing, 2004)

My Cat by Cate Foley (Children's Press, 2000)

My Dog by Sarah Hughes (Children's Press, 2001)

My Goldfish by Pamela Walker (Children's Press, 2001)

My Guinea Pig by Sarah Hughes (Children's Press, 2000)

My Parakeet by Pamela Walker (Children's Press, 2000)

My Turtle by Cate Foley (Children's Press, 2000)

Out and About at the Veterinary Clinic by Kitty Shea, illustrated by Becky Shipe (Picture Window Books, 2004)

Parrots and Parakeets as Pets by Elaine Landau (Children's Press, 1997)

Puppy by Honor Head, photographs by Jane Burton, illustrated by Pauline Bayne (Raintree Steck-Vaughn, 2001)

Puppy by Mark Evans (DK Publishing, 1992)

Puppy Care by Kim Dennis-Bryan (DK Publishing, 2004)

Rabbit by Honor Head, photographs by Jane Burton, illustrated by Pauline Bayne (Raintree Steck-Vaughn, 2001)

Rabbit by Mark Evans (Dorling Kindersley, 1992)

Rabbits by Michaela Miller (Heinemann Interactive Library, 1998)

Rats by June McNicholas (Heinemann Library, 2003)

Rats & Mice by Honor Head, photographs by Jane Burton, illustrated by Pauline Bayne (Raintree Steck-Vaughn, 2001)

Snakes by Sonia Hernandez-Divers (Heinemann Library, 2003)

Turtles by Ann Larkin Hansen (ABDO & Daughters, 1997)

We Work at the Vet's by Angela Aylmore (Raintree, 2006)

Why Do Cats Meow? by Joan Holub (Dial Books for Young Readers, 2001)

Why Do Rabbits Hop? And Other Questions About Rabbits, Guinea Pigs, Hamsters, and Gerbils by Joan Holub, illustrations by Anna DiVito (Dial Books for Young Readers, 2003)

Other Resources:

Children's print encyclopedias.

Mediated searches of online encyclopedias.

Databases and Web sites through mediated searches.

PROJECT TWO: *Bye-Bye Baby Teeth*

☆ Relevance

Grade one is typically the time that children begin to lose their baby teeth and have adult teeth grow in. This topic is highly relevant to children and they have many questions and misconceptions about the process. This process is the first big change that children experience in their development towards adulthood, and as such it is a topic that deserves attention. Medical facts about teeth and the process of growing into a whole new set can ease potential fears and embarrassment. Knowledge from books and experts will help children to take care of their teeth and understand potential problems that may need to be addressed.

💬 Discussion

Storybooks about losing baby teeth far outnumber nonfiction treatments of the subject. This is a shame because the whole process is quite fascinating. However, fiction can be a good method of beginning the discussion about such a project, especially as it deals with the worries that can loom large for children as their teeth begin to wiggle and come loose. Once they have had a chance to see how fictional children deal with this early milestone in their development, they will be able to move on to more scientific questions. Why does this happen? How does it happen? Which teeth fall out first? How long does it take for a tooth to fall out? Which teeth grow in first? How long does the process last? Should you pull at a tooth that is loose? Will the tooth fairy come? What will she leave? Why do some new teeth seem so big? What if a new tooth comes in crooked? Can crooked teeth straighten out? What happens if you have a baby tooth knocked out in an accident? When did your baby teeth first appear? Questions will be endless.

🔍 Investigation

Like most good projects, questions will be raised that teachers and librarians cannot answer. For this reason, the investigation should include visiting experts, nonfiction, and Web sites. Through their own experience, their exposure to stories, and knowledge from older friends and siblings, children will be bursting with questions on this subject. A dentist can address their concerns. Nonfiction can offer more information on the process and the care of both baby and adult teeth. Any remaining questions can be answered by Web sites from family health and parenting sites. Just as the librarian shares information from informational books, so too a Web site can be read to children or shared directly through an LCD projector.

▶ End Product

Potential end products for this topic are numerous. Children might write a story about their own experience with losing their baby teeth. Class charts measuring the progress of loose teeth could be filled in over the course of the entire school year. Instructive posters about tooth loss could be designed to share with younger students. The final product will undoubtedly be a stimulating combination of personal anecdote and new medical understanding.

 ## Resources for "Bye-Bye Baby Teeth"

Informative Fiction:

Amanda Pig and the Wiggly Tooth by Jean Van Leeuwen, illustrated by Ann Schweninger (Dial Books for Young Readers, 2007)

Andrew's Loose Tooth by Robert Munsch, illustrated by Michael Martchenko (Scholastic, 2002)

Arthur's Loose Tooth by Lillian Hoban (HarperTrophy, 1985)

Dad, Are You the Tooth Fairy? by Jason Alexander, illustrated by Ron Spears (Orchard Books, 2005)

Dear Tooth Fairy by Alan Durant, illustrated by Vanessa Cabban (Walker, 2003)

Dear Tooth Fairy by Karen Gray Ruelle (Holiday House, 2006)

Dear Tooth Fairy by Pamela Duncan Edwards, illustrated by Marie-Louise Fitzpatrick (Katherine Tegen Books, 2003)

Fluffy Meets the Tooth Fairy by Kate McMullan, illustrated by Mavis Smith (Scholastic, 2003)

Fooling the Tooth Fairy by Martin Nelson Burton, illustrated by Clint Hansen (London Town Press, 2005)

Franklin and the Tooth Fairy by Paulette Bourgeois, illustrated by Brenda Clark (Kids Can Press, 1995)

How Many Teeth? by Paul Showers, illustrated by True Kelly (HarperCollins, 1991)

I Lost a Tooth in Africa by Penda Diakité, illustrated by Baba Wagué Diakité (Scholastic, 2005)

I Want My Tooth by Tony Ross (Kane/Milled, 2002)

Loose Tooth by Anatasia Suen, illustrated by Allan Eitzen based on characters created by Ezra Jack Keats (Viking, 2002)

Loose Tooth by Lola Schaefer, illustrated by Sylvie Wickstrom (HarperCollins, 2004)

Loose-Tooth Luke by Patsy Jensen, illustrated by Dorothy Handelman (Millbrook Press, 1998)

Marissa the Tooth Fairy by Karla Margaret Andersdatter, illustrated by Deborah Koff (Depot Books, 2005)

My Loose Tooth by Stephen Krensky (Random House, 1999)

My Tooth Is About to Fall Out by Grace Maccarone, illustrated by Betsy Lewin (Scholastic, 2003)

My Tooth Is Loose by Susan Hood (Reader's Digest Children's Books, 1999)

Science Fair Bunnies by Kathryn Lasky, illustrated by Marylin Hafner (Candlewick Press, 2000)

The Lost Tooth Club by Arden Johnson-Petrov (Scholastic, 2004)

The Missing Tooth by Joanna Cole, illustrated by Marylin Hafner (Random House, 1988)

The Missing Tooth by Susan Blackaby, illustrated by Ryan Haugen (Picture Window Books, 2005)

The Mystery of the Missing Tooth by William H. Hooks, illustrated by Nancy Poydar (Gareth Stevens, 1998)

The Prince's Tooth Is Loose by Harriet Ziefert (Sterling, 2005)

The Prince's Tooth Is Loose by R. W. Alley (Sterling, 2005)

The Tooth Fairy by Kirsten Hall, illustrated by Dawn Apperley (Children's Press, 2003)

Tooth Fairy's First Night by Anne Bowen, illustrations by Jon Berkeley (Carolrhoda Books, 2005)

Tooth Trouble by Abby Klein, illustrated by John McKinley (Blue Sky Press, 2004)

Nonfiction:

A Look at Teeth by Allan Fowler (Children's Press, 1999)

A Tooth Is Loose by Lisa Trumbauer, illustrated by Steve Gray (Children's Press, 2004)

George Washington's Teeth by Deborah Chandra and Madeleine Comora, illustrated by Brock Cole (Scholastic, 2003)

Healthy Teeth by Angela Royston (Heinemann Library, 2003)

I Know Why I Brush My Teeth by Kate Rowan, illustrated by Katharine McEwen

Skin, Hair and Teeth by Neil Ardley

Teeth by Saviour Pirotta (Smart Apple Media, 2004)

Those Icky Sticky Smelly Cavity-Causing But-Invisible Germs by Judith Rice, illustrated by Julie Stricklin, photographs by Petronella J. Ytsma (Redleaf Press, 1997)

Throw Your Tooth on the Roof: Tooth Traditions from Around the World by Selby B. Beeler, illustrated by G. Brian Karas (Houghton Mifflin, 1998)

Why Should I Brush My Teeth?: And Other Questions About Healthy Teeth by Louise Spilsbury (Heinemann Library, 2003)

Your Teeth by Helen Frost (Pebble Books, 1999)

Easy Readers:

A Tooth Story by Margaret McNamara, illustrated by Mike Gordon (Scholastic, 2004)

Dear Tooth Fairy by Jane O'Connor, illustrated by Joy Allen (Grosset & Dunlap, 2002)

Loose Tooth by Anastasia Suen and Allan Eitzen, illustrated by Ezra Jack Keats (Viking, 2002)

Supertwins and Tooth Trouble by B.J. James, illustrated by Chris Demarest (Scholastic, 2003)

Longer Books for Read-Alouds:

Agapanthus Hum and the Angel Hoot by Joy Cowley, illustrated by Jennifer Plecas (Philomel Books, 2003)

Junie B., First Grader: Toothless Wonder by Barbara Park, illustrated by Denise Brunkus (Random House, 2002)

Horrid Henry Tricks the Tooth Fairy by Francesca Simon (Orion, 2005)

Young Cam Jansen and the Lost Tooth by David A. Adler, illustrated by Susanna Natti (Viking, 1997)

Other Resources:

Mediated searches of Web sites.

Mediated searches of children's databases.

PROJECT THREE: *Jobs at School*

 ## Relevance

Children know most of the names of people who work at the school, but they may not understand what they do. The project approach to jobs at school allows children to get out of the classroom and into direct contact with people they might never have had the chance to talk to or question. Secretaries, cafeteria workers, custodians, librarians, bus drivers, nurses, counselors, psychologists, principals, and even teachers have something to tell children about the jobs that they do and their roles in the life of the school. Just because children see these people everyday does not mean that they understand their function in the school. Because the children will have questions about people who play a part in their everyday lives, this is a relevant and worthwhile project.

 ## Discussion

Many stories have been written, both serious and silly, about the people who work in a school. The librarian can get the ball rolling with stories, but it is also a good idea to have the gym teacher, principal, or custodian share stories and nonfiction as well. Having particular people read these stories to children – especially when they are stories that poke gentle fun at stereotypes – is sure to make the project seem more appealing. Have these teachers visit the library to share in a discussion about the book that deals with their particular job. While the teacher is answering questions, the librarian can begin taking notes that will drive the investigation.

 ## Investigation

Dividing students into groups can make the investigation more manageable. Children can begin to consider questions for interviews by examining a K-W-L chart about the various jobs within the school. How much do they really know about what each job entails? What else would they like to know? After hearing and reading nonfiction about these jobs, do they have further questions to add under "W"?

 ## End Product

Parents are crucial to the interview stage of the project since it will require children to be at various locations throughout the school. Parents can use digital camcorders to record the interview or note the answers of each expert. Often children will need prompting and assistance in formulating their questions, even though they have been prepared beforehand. These videos or notes would then become the material for their end product to show what they have learned.

Resources for "Jobs at School"

Stories:

First Day, Hooray! by Nancy Poydar (Holiday House, 1999)

First Day Jitters by Julie Danneberg, illustrated by Judy Love (Whispering Coyote by Charlesbridge, 2000)

Library Lil by Suzanne Williams, illustrated by Steven Kellogg (Dial Books For Young Readers, 1997)

Lilly's Purple Plastic Purse by Kevin Henkes (Greenwillow Books, 1996)

The A+ Custodian by Louise Borden, illustrated by Adam Gustavson (Margaret K. McElderry Books, 2004)

The Cafeteria Lady from the Black Lagoon by Mike Thaler, illustrated by Jared Lee (Scholastic, 1998)

The Day the Teacher Went Bananas by James Howe, illustrated by Lillian Hoban (Dutton Children's Books, 1984)

The Frog Principal by Stephanie Calmenson, illustrated by Denise Brunkus (Scholastic, 2001)

The Librarian from the Black Lagoon by Mike Thaler, illustrated by Jared Lee (Scholastic, 1997)

The Music Teacher from the Black Lagoon by Mike Thaler, illustrated by Jared Lee (Scholastic, 2000)

The Principal from the Black Lagoon by Mike Thaler, illustrated by Jared Lee (Scholastic, 1993)

The School Bus Driver from the Black Lagoon by Mike Thaler, illustrated by Jared Lee (Scholastic, 1999)

The School Nurse from the Black Lagoon by Mike Thaler, illustrated by Jared Lee (Scholastic, 1995)

The Teacher from the Black Lagoon by Mike Thaler, illustrated by Jared Lee (Scholastic, 1989)

What Teachers Can't Do by Douglas Wood, illustrated by Doug Cushman (Simon & Schuster Books for Young Readers, 2002)

Poems:

The Bug in Teacher's Coffee and Other School Poems by Kalli Dakos, illustrated by Mike Reed (HarperTrophy, 1999)

Nonfiction:

Custodians by Robin Nelson, photographs by Stephen G. Donaldson (Lerner, 2005)

I Want to Be a Teacher by Dan Liebman (Firefly Books, 2001)

Meet My Teacher by Elizabeth Vogel (PowerKids Press, 2002)

Meet the Cafeteria Workers by Elizabeth Vogel (PowerKids Press, 2002)

Meet the Librarian by Elizabeth Vogel (PowerKids Press, 2002)

Meet the Principal by Elizabeth Vogel (PowerKids Press, 2002)

Meet the School Nurse by Elizabeth Vogel (PowerKids Press, 2002)

Meet the School Secretary by Elizabeth Vogel (PowerKids Press, 2002)

Principals by Melanie Mitchell, photographs by Stephen G. Donaldson (Lerner, 2005)

School Bus Drivers by Dee Ready (Bridgestone Books, 1998)

School Bus Drivers by Melanie Mitchell, photographs by Jim Baron (Lerner, 2005)

T Is for Teachers: A School Alphabet by Steven L. Layne and Deborah Dover Layne, illustrated by Doris Ettlinger (Sleeping Bear, 2005)

Teacher by Heather Miller (Heinemann Library, 2003)

Teachers by Charnan Simon (Child's World, 2003)

Teachers by Melanie Mitchell (Lerner, 2005)

That's Our Custodian! by Ann Morris, illustrated by Peter Linenthal (Millbrook Press, 2003)

That's Our Gym Teacher! by Ann Morris, illustrated by Peter Linenthal (Millbrook Press, 2003)

That's Our Librarian! by Ann Morris, illustrated by Peter Linenthal (Millbrook Press, 2003)

That's Our Nurse! by Ann Morris, illustrated by Peter Linenthal (Millbrook Press, 2003)

That's Our Principal! by Ann Morris, illustrated by Peter Linenthal (Millbrook Press, 2003)

We Need Custodians by Jane Scoggins Bauld (Pebble Books, 2000)

We Need Librarians by Jane Scoggins Bauld (Pebble Books, 2000)

We Need Principals by Jane Scoggins Bauld (Pebble Books, 2000)

We Need School Bus Drivers by Helen Frost (Capstone Press, 2005)

We Need Teachers by Jane Scoggins Bauld (Pebble Books, 2000)

What Is a Teacher? by Barbara Lehn, photographs by Carol Krauss (Millbrook, 2000)

Who's Who in a School Community by Jake Miller (PowerKids Press, 2005)

PROJECT FOUR: *Growing Plants*

 Relevance

Learning about plants by planting seeds and helping them to grow gives children essential hands-on experience that in turn helps to create interest and make the topic relevant to them. Children probably have some knowledge and even experience with gardening already, and they should be encouraged to share their stories and observations.

 Discussion

Initiate discussion for this project with informative stories and nonfiction in the library. These dialogic readings will ensure that those without direct experience pick up some ideas and vocabulary before the investigation stage. In this way the librarian can ensure that all students will be ready to join in class discussions about plans for experimentation and possible research questions that may be answered by these experiments.

 Investigation

Some of the best plants to grow for such a project are runner beans because they are easy to plant and they grow quickly, thus making them suitable for young children. Many of the nonfiction books listed here about how to plant seeds deal explicitly with beans. Thus, both children and teacher will be well prepared to plant beans and take care of them as they make observations about how plants grow and what they need to remain healthy.

Children will have suggestions about what they will need before they have read instructions in information books. These should be noted beforehand. As the children read and are read more about plants, they may add to their list of materials and instructions. Once they have established clear guidelines, they are ready to tackle the actual planting and make up a schedule for watering. Questions and predictions about the plant's growth should be noted now. These preliminary notes will help develop focus for the project and its outcome.

Once the beans are planted, the investigation will begin in earnest. If children are interested in knowing how much sun or water is best for the beans, their teacher can help them to experiment with the beans and to figure out ways of noting their observations for use later on.

 End Product

As data are collected, children can decide what format their end product will take. Perhaps they will write a book about each experimental planting. Maybe they will make posters of observations and conclusions. If a digital camera is used to monitor the growth, a photo essay on each experiment is a possibility.

Meanwhile, children can continue to have questions answered and develop new insights in their library sessions. How do beans compare to other plants? How many types of beans are there? Why do people have gardens? What kinds of plants do people like to grow? How do plants grow on their own without anyone to help them? These and other questions can be explored in their library sessions and then added to their final product.

 ## Resources for "Growing Plants"

Informative Stories:

A Gardener's Alphabet by Mary Azarian (Houghton Mifflin, 2000)

And the Good Brown Earth by Kathy Henderson (Candlewick Press, 2004)

A Place to Grow by Soyung Pak, illustrated by Marcelino Truong (Arthur Levine, 2002)

Eddie's Garden and How to Make Things Grow by Sarah Garland (Frances Lincoln Children's Books, 2004)

Flower Garden by Eve Bunting, illustrated by Kathryn Hewitt (Harcourt Brace, 1994)

Fluffy Grows a Garden by Kate McMullan, illustrated by Mavis Smith (Scholastic, 2001)

Growing Vegetable Soup by Lois Ehlert (Harcourt Brace, 1987)

I'm a Seed by Jean Marzollo, illustrated by Judith Moffatt (Scholastic, 1996)

Jack's Garden by Henry Cole (Greenwillow Books, 1995)

Jody's Beans by Malachy Doyle, illustrated by Judith Allibone (Candlewick Press, 1999)

Johnny Appleseed by Patricia Demuth, illustrated by Michael Montgomery (Grosset & Dunlap, 1996)

Lily's Garden by Deborah Kogan Ray (Roaring Brook Press, 2002)

Ten Seeds by Ruth Brown (Alfred A. Knopf, 2001)

The Carrot Seed by Ruth Krauss, illustrated by Crockett Johnson (Harper & Brothers, 1945)

The Tiny Seed by Eric Carle (Simon & Schuster Books for Young Readers, 1987 reissue of the original 1970 edition, with expanded collage illustrations)

The Ugly Vegetables by Grace Lin (Talewinds/Charlesbridge, 1999)

Stories:

Carrot Soup by Margaret K. McElderry, 2006)

Flora's Surprise! by Debi Gliori (Orchard Books, 2002)

Koa's Seed: A Hawaiian Version of an Age-Old Tale retold by Carolyn Han, illustrated by Kathleen Peterson (BeachHouse Publishing, 2004)

Muncha, Muncha, Muncha by Candace Fleming, illustrated by Brian G. Karas (Atheneum Books for Young Readers, 2002)

Sunflower by Miela Ford, illustrated by Sally Noll (Greenwillow, 1995)

The Gardener by Sarah Stewart, illustrated by David Small (Farrar, Straus & Giroux, 1997)

The Little Red Hen Makes a Pizza retold by Philemon Sturges, illustrated by Amy Walrod (Dutton Children's Books, 1999)

The Pea Blossom retold and illustrated by Amy Lowry Poole (Holiday House, 2005)

Tops and Bottoms by Janet Stevens (Harcourt Brace, 1995)

Poems, Riddles, and Rhymes:

Busy in the Garden (Greenwillow, 2006)

The Garden That We Grew by Joan Holub, illustrations by Hiroe Nakata (Viking, 2001)

Vegetable Garden by Douglas Florian (Harcourt Brace Jovanovich, 1996)

Nonfiction:

A Harvest of Color: Growing a Vegetable Garden by Melanie Eclare (Ragged Bears, 2002)

A Kid's Guide to How Fruit Grows by Patricia Ayers (PowerKids Press, 2000)

A Kid's Guide to How Herbs Grow by Patricia Ayers (PowerKids Press, 2000)

A Kid's Guide to How Trees Grow by Patricia Ayers (PowerKids Press, 2000)

A Kid's Guide to How Vegetables Grow by Patricia Ayers (PowerKids Press, 2000)

A Parade of Plants by Melissa Stewart (Compass Point Books, 2004)

Apples by Inez Snyder (Children's Press, 2004)

Apples by Ken Robbins (Atheneum Books for Young Readers, 2002)

Apples: And How They Grow by Laura Driscoll, illustrated by Tammy Smith (Grosset & Dunlap, 2003)

Bean by Louise Spilsbury (Heinemann Library, 2005)

Beans by Gail Saunders-Smith (Pebble Books, 1998)

Beans by Joyce Bentley (Smart Apple Media, 2006)

Beans by Melanie Mitchell (Lerner, 2003)

Blue Potatoes, Orange Tomatoes by Rosalind Creasy, illustrated by Ruth Heller (Sierra Club Books for Children, 1994)

Carrots by Gail Saunders-Smith (Pebble Books, 1998)

Carrots by Inez Snyder (Children's Press, 2004)

Children's Book of Yoga: Games & Exercises Mimic Plants & Animals & Objects by Thia Luby (Clear Light Publishers, 1998)

Flowers, Fruits and Seeds by Angela Royston (Heinemann Library, 1999)

From Blossom to Fruit by Gail Saunders-Smith (Pebble Books, 1998)

From Seed to Plant by Allan Fowler (Children's Press, 2001)

From Seed to Plant by Gail Gibbons (Holiday House, 1991)

From Seed to Pumpkin by Jan Kottke, photographs by Dwight Kuhn (Children's Press, 2000)

From Shoot to Apple by Stacy Taus-Bolstad (Lerner, 2003)

Garden by Robert Maass (Henry Holt, 1998)

Growing Herbs by Tracy Nelson Maurer (Rourke Book Co., 2001)

How Plants Grow by Angela Royston (Heinemann Library, 1999)

Life Cycle of a Pumpkin by Ron Fridell and Patricia Walsh, illustrated by David Westerfield (Heinemann Library, 2001)

Life of a Sunflower by Clare Hibbert (Raintree, 2004)

My Indoor Garden by Carol Lerner (HarperCollins, 1999)

Oak Trees by Melanie Mitchell (Lerner, 2003)

One Bean by Anne Rockwell, illustrated by Megan Halsey (Walker, 1998)

Plant Growth by Richard and Louise Spilsbury, illustrated by Jeff Edwards

Potatoes by Melanie Mitchell (Lerner, 2003)

Scholastic's the Magic School Bus Plants Seeds by Patricia Relf and Joanna Cole, illustrated by John Speirs (Scholastic, 1995)

The Gardening Book by Jane Bull, photographs by Andy Crawford (DK Publishing, 2003)

The Life of a Bean by Clare Hibbert (Raintree, 2005)

The Pumpkin Patch by Elizabeth King (Orchard, 1993)

Tomatoes by Inez Snyder (Children's Press, 2004)

Tulips by Melanie Mitchell (Lerner, 2003)

Vegetables, Vegetables! by Fay Robinson (Children's Press, 1994)

We Love Fruit! by Fay Robinson (Children's Press, 1992)

Videos:

Fruit [videorecording] by Andrew C. Sullivan, Katie Thatcher (BFA Educational Media, 2003, 10 min.)

Pumpkin Circle [videorecording] written and directed by George Levenson (Informed Democracy, 1997, 20 min.)

The Gardener [videorecording] by Sarah Stewart, illustrated by David Small (Live Oak Media, 1998, 11 min.)

Chapter Seven

Research and Inquiry in Grade Two

Working With Children in Grade Two

The last year of what is considered to belong to early childhood education is a year of transitions. Children engaging in project work will be more self-directed than ever before. Making decisions and working in small groups will be easier than ever before. These children are now all readers and thus will be able to handle more text on their own, with help from the teacher and librarian, rather than be read to. However, dialogic reading still has a place in second grade projects. Working with small groups, a librarian can still question and help guide students to tackle information sources for answers to their questions. Online as well, children of this age need a lot of scaffolding if they are to succeed in locating information that will answer their needs – both in terms of content and readability.

Children of this age still need lots of hands-on experience. This aspect of project work should not be abandoned because the children can now read to gain information. Connections between what they read and their own experience are still essential for real learning to take place.

Seven-year-olds have come a long way socially. Listening and sharing skills are well developed. Seven-year-olds will negotiate within their group and come to agreement on how to organize and divide their work. Of course, an adult facilitator is still necessary to help them learn about roles within a group.

By the time children are eight years old they have real curiosity about the world. A wide variety of topics will hold their interest – from other parts of the world to other parts of the universe. Their ability to reason and their growing fund of knowledge will ensure that they take on projects of their own in their spare time. This love of learning for its own sake has been fostered by the project approach and their early exposure to the pleasures and rewards of nonfiction. These children are now true researchers and inquirers.

Informational Strategies in Grade Two

Children in grade two are ready for fairly advanced exploration of nonfiction sources. As their questions grow in number and complexity, mediated searches of Internet and children's online databases will become necessary to answer some questions.

- Children are asked to differentiate between how a story is read (beginning, middle, end) and how an informational book is used (choosing the section of the book that will answer the question).
- Children recognize that a difficult informational book might still convey information through pictures, photographs, diagrams, and charts.
- Children use highlighter tape to highlight key words in a table of contents that relate to their questions.
- Children use a table of contents in short informational books (around 32 pages) to find chapters that answer their questions.
- Children highlight keywords in their own student-generated questions, with the help of the teacher or librarian.
- Teachers and librarians ask children to find keywords from a simple index using a projection from an informational e-book.
- Children use highlighter tape to highlight key terms in simple indexes of short informational books.
- Children use terms to describe elements of an informational book, such as table of contents, chapter, page number, heading, paragraph, photograph, image, chart, diagram, caption, and boxed text.
- Children analyze page layout from an age-appropriate informational book, identifying which parts go together by circling and cutting from photocopied pages (heading with paragraph, caption with heading, boxed text, diagram, or chart).
- Children use headings, captions, and charts in their own informational products.
- Children are asked to articulate what kinds of informational books they like to read and why.
- Children are made aware of the sections of the nonfiction collection by exploring their favorite nonfiction books.

Projects

PROJECT ONE: *My Five Senses*

 ## Relevance

Left on their own to come up with a topic for investigation, children might not think of their five senses. Yet this subject is rich in possibilities for scientific experimentation suitable to young children. This, coupled with the wide variety of age-appropriate resources on this topic, makes it a relevant choice for young learners. Previous projects from the early years about "My Hands" and "Taste and Smell" have already given the children some hands-on exploration of their senses. Now they are ready for a more in-depth examination of the science behind the senses.

 ## Discussion

Children use their five senses every day without really thinking about them. To stimulate interest in something that they have taken for granted for most of their lives, the teacher can invite them to try some simple experiments with her. She might tell the children that she was reading some interesting books in the school library and would like to test some of the experiments with the children. *Sense-abilities: Fun Ways to Explore the Senses*, *Experiment with Senses*, *The Five Senses* (from the "It's Science" series), and *My Science Book of Senses* all have easy and fun experiments that the children would have no trouble replicating. This hands-on approach is a surefire way to kick off a discussion about a science-based project.

The library media specialist can follow up the classroom experiments with an examination of the library books. Show the children the books and pages where these experiments were found. Once children embark on "My Five Senses" as a project, they will need to know how to search for experiments of their own to try. Show them the steps to follow: finding a word in the table of contents or index, examining the picture of the experiment, reading the caption (with headings such as "Try It Out") or explanation (with a list of materials and numbered step-by-step instructions), and finally deciding whether or not these experiments are doable. Going through this process of reading the text in a dialogic reading using CROWD questions will give children an opportunity to see the use of an informational book modeled. ("What is the boy in the picture doing?" "How is he holding the card?" "What do you think will happen?" "Could we try this experiment now?" "Who would like to try this and who would like to make observations?") In pairs, have the children search for experiments themselves and evaluate whether or not the descriptions and pictures make it seem doable. Those pairs who wish to share their findings should be allowed to do so before the end of the library session.

Back in the classroom, the teacher can ask the children to arrange themselves into five groups of similar size. Self-selecting their own groups gives children the opportunity to choose classmates with whom they are comfortable working. However, if there are potential problems grouping certain children together or if there are children who are often left out of self-selected groups, it is best for the teacher to choose the groups. Teachers who know their students well may prefer to group children in a way that will distribute certain strengths and abilities to each group.

Provide each group with materials as each experiment is explained, making sure that there are enough materials for all the children to be involved. As each experiment is demonstrated, ask them to predict what they think will happen. Then get them to try it themselves and report their findings to the class. Ask them what sense they have used after each experiment is complete. Use this as an opportunity to discover how much vocabulary and understanding they already have relating to their senses.

To demonstrate something about sight, the teacher might ask the children to close one eye and then try to put the cap on a pen or marker as the boy on page 10 of *The Five Senses* is doing. Which is easier – with one eye open or two? Why? To investigate hearing, the children might make a noise with an object and get their friends to guess what it is as on page 12 of *The Five Senses*. For the sense of touch, the children could make fingerprints and compare them under a magnifying glass, as explained on page 21 of *Experiment with Senses*. Are they all the same or different? The sense of taste and smell could be examined by inviting a volunteer to come up to the front of the class to taste various kinds of fruit juice, as the instructions on page 24 and 25 of *My Science Book of Senses* describes. Can he identify the juices with a blindfold on? What if he plugs his nose?

Ask the children what explanations they can offer about each of the experiments. Note their answers on the board for each of the sensory experiments. Ask them if they would be interested in doing some experimenting of the five senses themselves. Get them to think about questions that they could ask for each different sense and note these as a web on separate sheets of large paper. These can be given to the groups afterwards as a basis for further thinking about what questions their project will attempt to answer. Ask them to think about the kind of end product that they could produce if they studied the five senses as a project. The children will have no trouble coming up with ideas based on their previous experience of projects. One likely idea would be a "Discovery Center for the 5 Senses," especially if the children have previously visited a hands-on museum or science center for children. Get the children to come up with a name for the center and to decide who their target audience will be.

Once the children are convinced that the project is doable and interesting enough for a sustained project, it is time to assign a sense to each group. The children are already in groups. Making a game out of the selection of senses can help avoid battles over which group gets which sense if resources are limited. Nothing prevents groups from doing the same sense, but it is important that all the senses are studied. The children will likely insist that their science center has to cover all the senses.

To further their thinking during Phase One, the librarian might read a book that deals with all the senses. A title such as *You Can't Smell a Flower With Your Ear* is a good choice. This book covers fairly complex scientific information about the five senses in clearly written prose. If the class needs an easier introduction to the senses, Allan Fowler's series would be a good place to start. These make excellent books for dialogic reading since they have questions throughout and naturally will invite comment from the children as you read. A video such as *Our Five Senses* will help children to acquire more vocabulary and special terms, thus furthering their generation of questions and ideas for the project. This 15 minute DVD handles the related topics of blindness and deafness well, which may in turn stimulate questions. If questions do arise or the children do not seem to have had much contact with people with visual or hearing impairments, there are many good stories that deal with these topics. The "Resources" section at the end of this chapter lists four books about seeing-eye dogs, deafness, and prescription eyeglasses.

Now the children can complete Phase One by making crucial decisions about the project.

1. Questions on their web. Have they added all of the questions that they can think of to the web diagram for their sense? Can they decide which questions are most important?

2. End products. What will they need to produce so that visitors to their discovery center can learn about the five senses? Children will likely decide on an experiment that the visitors can try themselves and a poster explaining how to do the experiment step-by-step. Another possibility is to develop a question and answer book or fact sheet about their sense. The product is up to the child, but it is important that the teacher and librarian encourage them to share the answers to their questions in some format.

3. Models. Once the end products have been decided upon, the children need to find a model of each product that they can follow. Perhaps a visit to a science discovery center will be necessary. Or, the teacher might volunteer to design samples herself of step-by-step instructions and fact sheets. Or, the class can visit an upper elementary class to look at examples of their work on scientific experimentation. This is a chance for the teacher to make suggestions to assist the students in coming up with plans that are doable. For instance, a procedure sheet might involve too much writing for grade two students to handle. The teacher might suggest that they use the class digital camera to take pictures of themselves performing each step. Then all the pictures need are short captions. Any further explanations will be given orally by the students when their science discovery center opens.

4. Evaluating their end products. Children should devise their own guidelines for the way end products will look. The teacher should note all of their suggestions on a poster board that the children can then refer to as they work on their final products. Simple rubrics can be drawn up that make statements about the work, such as "Instructions are numbered and easy to follow." "The fact sheet or booklet has five interesting facts about the sense we have chosen." "The fact sheet or booklet should contain at least one diagram or drawing."

5. Timeline. The children should also be involved in making up a plan for the duration of the project. How many classes do they think they will need in the library? Are there some materials that they will need to bring from home?

6. Roles. Finally, children need to be clear about who does what. If their fact sheets will have drawings, someone who likes to draw can volunteer for that. Everyone needs to have a part in the end product and in the final display phase when they must help visitors understand what they have developed.

 ## Investigation

Now it is time for Phase Two. This is a project where the investigation phase is based largely on library research to get their information. The project has already been defined and questions have been developed. So children will first need help with locating resources.

Children should come to the library with their web diagrams. These can be placed on their group's table for consultation as they research. The librarian should have each group develop a search card. This will guide them to resources and help them to scan for important words. Students should be asked to write the Dewey number for the senses (612.8) at the top of the card. This will get them to the right area with the help of the librarian. Next they should list all the words that might be used to describe their sense. For example, if they are doing "taste" the book title might use the words taste, tasting, or mouth. A book about touch might use hands, fingers, touch, touching, feel, or feeling. These are now their "keywords." Keywords will help them locate information in print sources and will be useful again to search electronic sources. Group by group, children can go to the medical section of the library to find books about their particular sense. Afterwards, one member of each group can go to the shelves again to find books about *all* the senses. These resources can then circulate among all the groups.

The first library class should have as its goal the location of an experiment that the children will prepare for their discovery center. With the help of the teacher and the librarian, the children can decide on an experiment that is both interesting and feasible. Then they can figure out what materials they will need and who will collect what.

On the back of their search card they should write the title of the book and the name of the author. Children will need to be told that they must tell visitors to the discovery center where they found their experiment. So the teacher will now add a statement about sources to their evaluation guidelines: "The experiment poster includes a note at the bottom about where the experiment was taken from, including the title of the book and the author's name." All the books that children have selected as important to their project will now be placed on reserve for future use.

After the first library class, the project will continue in the classroom as they put together their poster and create any special constructions necessary to their experiment. During this work, questions should continue to come up as the children try the experiment themselves. Some ideas may need to be verified and new information found. When questions arise, it is a good indication that it is time for another trip to the library.

The gathering of information for the fact booklet and answers to questions that have come up may take several library periods to complete. Students should work in pairs for this activity since it will require closer reading of books and other sources. Each pair should have one question written at the top of a note-taking card or should simply write "My Fact About Taste" at the top if they will be looking for information to include in the fact booklet. Students at this age are often more comfortable taking notes with lines on the paper. Lined index cards or paper can be provided, with plain paper available for diagrams or drawings.

▶ End Product

At this stage, as they are developing the content for their end products, there will be many more information needs than there were in the first library class. Both teacher and librarian will have to help students with their reading, decision-making, and note-taking in their own words. Again, each time a question or fact card is filled out, the source should be written on the back of the card. As with the experiment poster, the fact booklet or sheet needs to include a statement about where the information was found. This too will have to be added to the evaluation rubric. Students will now have an opportunity to explore online databases and encyclopedias for information if they are not satisfied with the information in the books.

The K-5 subscription database from Thomson Gale, *Kids InfoBits*, can be searched for the subject "senses," but children will need assistance discriminating between articles about animal senses and those dealing with human senses. Children will also need help in choosing an easy article. Even these may be difficult for some grade two readers, so library media specialists may prefer to pre-select the articles by printing them or using "infomarks." In many cases, articles are accompanied by interesting images and photographs, which will aid children in interpreting the content. Children should be encouraged to read out the title and the brief description that is often given in parentheses afterwards. These clues can help the students reject some articles immediately, for instance those that are poems, letters, or writing exercises.

Once their information has been gathered, the children can begin work on their booklets. Library computers may be used for typing up their facts or the children might wish to create something by hand. The choice should be theirs. As follow-up to these research periods, a few children may have to come back for further verification or answers as they continue work on their project in the class.

 ## Integrating Standards

As with the project "Animal Friends," this project is first and foremost about science. Taking Arizona's state standards as an example, most of the components of the science standard are met. Strand One, "Inquiry Process," is clearly met by the process of experimentation involving observations, questions, and predictions plus planning investigations, noting data, and communicating results. Strand Two, "Nature of Science," is met as the children identify parts within each sense organ. Strand Three, "Science in Personal and Social Perspectives" is covered as children examine how technologies can be used to assist people with disabilities. Strand Four, related to life sciences, is clearly in evidence as children explore the structure and function of sense organs. Recording data and making observations inevitably involve mathematics concepts as well. Findings from experimentation can be presented using charts and graphs. Standards related to problem solving, representation, and measurement are likely to be met.

Despite the scientific focus, this project has elements of other content-area standards as well. Literacy standards are in evidence throughout the project as students listen to stories and read informational books. Dispositions, such as persistence and curiosity, are necessary to a project based on experimentation. For this project to succeed, children must possess the social and emotional competencies required by group work. Even social studies standards can be met here as children become aware of figures who have contributed to our understanding of disabilities. Once again, the project approach to learning has proved to be a good fit with curriculum standards.

 ## Resources for "My Five Senses"

Books with Experiments:

Experimenting With Senses by Monica Byles, photographs by Paul Bricknell, illustrations by Nancy Anderson (Lerner Publications, 1994)

Feeling With the Fingers: How You Touch, Sense and Feel by Steve Parker (Franklin Watts, 1992)

How Do Our Ears Hear? by Carol Ballard (Raintree Steck-Vaughn, 1998)

How Do Our Eyes See? by Carol Ballard (Raintree Steck-Vaughn, 1998)

How Do We Feel and Touch? by Carol Ballard (Raintree Steck-Vaughn, 1998)

How Do We Taste and Smell? by Carol Ballard (Raintree Steck-Vaughn, 1998)

My Science Book of Senses by Neil Ardley (DK Publishing, 1992)

The Five Senses by Sally Hewitt (Children's Press, 1999)

Sense-Abilities: Fun Ways to Explore the Senses – Activities for Children 4 to 8 by Michelle O'Brien-Palmer (Chicago Review Books, 1998)

You Can't Smell a Flower With Your Ear by Joanna Cole (Grosset & Dunlap, 1994)

Poems:

Voices From the Wild: An Animal Sensagoria by Dave Bouchard, illustrated by Ron Parker (Chronicle Books, 1996)

Informational Book Read Aloud:

You Can't Smell a Flower With Your Ear by Joanna Cole (Grosset & Dunlap, 1994)

Videos:

Our Five Senses [videorecording] (100% Educational Videos, 2003 – June 2005 release DVD, 15 min.)

The Fabulous Five: Our Senses [videorecording] by Peter Cochran (Rainbow Educational Video, 1989)

Stories and Information Books About Visual and Hearing Impairment:

Buddy, the First Seeing Eye Dog by Eva Moore, illustrated by Don Bolognese (Scholastic, 1996)

Deafness by Angela Royston (Heinemann Library, 2005)

First Signs by Tina Jo Breindel, illustrated by Michael Carter (Dawnsign Press, 2005)

Let's Eat by Tina Jo Breindel, illustrated by Michael Carter (Dawnsign Press, 2005)

Listen for the Bus: David's Story by Patricia McMahon, photographs by John Godt (Boyds Mills Press, 1995)

Looking Out for Sarah by Glenna Lang (Talewinds, 2001)

Mandy Sue Day by Roberta Karim, illustrated by Karen Ritz (Clarion Books, 1994)

Moses Goes to a Concert by Isaac Millman (Frances Foster Books, 1998)

The Touch Me Book [print and Braille] by Pat Witte and Eve Witte, illustrated by Harlow Rockwell (Western Publishing Co., 1990)

Watch Out, Ronald Morgan by Patricia Reilly Giff, illustrated by Susanna Natti (Puffin, 1986)

Word Signs: A First Book of Sign Language by Debby Slier (Kendall Green Publications, 1995)

Information Books for Research:

Animal Senses: How Animals See, Hear, Taste, Smell, and Feel by Pamela Hickman, illustrated by Pat Stephens (Kids Can Press, 1998)

Hearing by Angela Royston (Chrysalis Education, 2005)

Hearing by Lillian Wright (Raintree Steck-Vaughn, 1995)

Hearing: A True Book by Patricia J. Murphy (Children's Press, 2003)

How Do Our Ears Hear? by Carol Ballard (Raintree Steck-Vaughn, 1998)

How Do Our Eyes See? by Carol Ballard (Raintree Steck-Vaughn, 1998)

How Do We Feel and Touch? by Carol Ballard (Raintree Steck-Vaughn, 1998)

How Do We Taste and Smell? by Carol Ballard (Raintree Steck-Vaughn, 1998)

How Your Senses Work by Jaime Ripoli, illustrations by Marcel Socías (Chelsea House Publishers, 1994)

Seeing by Lillian Wright (Raintree Steck-Vaughn, 1995)

Sight: A True Book by Patricia J. Murphy (Children's Press, 2003)

Smell: A True Book by Patricia J. Murphy (Children's Press, 2003)

Taste: A True Book by Patricia J. Murphy (Children's Press, 2003)

The Crazy and Amazing Five Senses Book by Nancy Snipper (Guérin, 1997)

The Five Senses by Sally Hewitt (Children's Press, 1999)

The Science of Senses by Patricia L. Miller-Schroeder (Weigl, 2000)

Touch: A True Book by Patricia J. Murphy (Children's Press, 2003)

Use Your Senses by Melissa Stewart (Compass Point Books, 2004)

Wow!: The Most Interesting Book You'll Ever Read About the Five Senses by Trudee Romanek, illustrated by Rose Cowles (Kids Can Press, 2004)

You Can't Smell a Flower With Your Ear by Joanna Cole (Grosset & Dunlap, 1994)

Easy Information Books for Research:

Feeling Things by Allan Fowler (Children's Press, 1991)

Hearing Things by Allan Fowler (Children's Press, 1991)

My Ears by Lloyd G. Douglas (Children's Press, 2003)

My Eyes by Lloyd G. Douglas (Children's Press, 2003)

My Hands by Lloyd G. Douglas (Children's Press, 2004)

My Mouth by Lloyd G. Douglas (Children's Press, 2004)

My Nose by Lloyd G. Douglas (Children's Press, 2003)

Seeing Things by Allan Fowler (Children's Press, 1991)

Smelling Things by Allan Fowler (Children's Press, 1991)

Tasting Things by Allan Fowler (Children's Press, 1991)

Think About Hearing by Henry Pluckrose, photographs by Chris Fairclough (Gareth Stevens, 1995 reissue)

Think About Seeing by Henry Pluckrose, photographs by Chris Fairclough (Gareth Stevens, 1995 reissue)

Think About Smelling by Henry Pluckrose, photographs by Chris Fairclough (Gareth Stevens, 1995 reissue)

Think About Tasting by Henry Pluckrose, photographs by Chris Fairclough (Gareth Stevens, 1995 reissue)

Think About Touching by Henry Pluckrose, photographs by Chris Fairclough (Gareth Stevens, 1995 reissue)

What Can I— Feel by Sue Barraclough (Raintree, 2005)

You Can't Taste a Pickle With Your Ear: A Book About Your Five Senses by Harriet Ziefert, illustrated by Amanda Haley (Blue Apple Books, 2002)

Encyclopedias:

Childcraft: The How and Why Library (World Book, 2000)

My First Britannica (Encyclopedia Britannica, 2004)

Oxford First Encyclopedia (Oxford University Press, 1998)

The New Grolier Encyclopedia (Grolier, 1998)

The Wonderful World of Knowledge (Grolier, 1999)

The World Book Student Discovery Encyclopedia (World Book, 2000)

Databases:

Kids InfoBits (Thomson Gale)

Primary Search with Searchasaurus (EBSCO)

Pre-selected Web sites if necessary.

PROJECT TWO: *Forecasting the Weather*

☆ Relevance

Children in grade two can understand much more about weather patterns than they did back in pre-kindergarten. Weather forecasters will be familiar from local and national television programs. Children are keen to hear about tomorrow's weather predictions when they have special outings planned. News of a coming blizzard will be greeted with anticipation of the fun to be had on a snow day. Weather forecasts affect their lives and thus weather is relevant as a project topic. But more than that, the technical aspects of weather forecasting and the notion of acting like a TV presenter are inherently interesting for children of this age.

⊙ Discussion

This project will begin with a discussion of what the children already know about forecasting the weather. From television they will be familiar with satellite images of clouds or tropical storms. Ask them to recall TV footage of extreme weather conditions, such as hurricanes or heavy snows. Children may be familiar with folk sayings or beliefs about how to predict the weather. As their ideas are noted by the teacher, questions or gaps in their knowledge will arise as well. These too should be noted for the upcoming project.

⚲ Investigation

Resources for this project include excellent nonfiction and video recordings about weather forecasting, plus some fun stories as well. These sources, shared in the classroom and library, can help children become motivated about the subject and increase their knowledge as they think about further questions to ask local experts. Knowing that they are preparing for a visit to a real meteorologist will make their use of information sources more meaningful. The investigation could include other experts as well, such as people with knowledge of traditional ways of predicting the weather.

▶ End Product

Children may be interested in presenting their research findings as a television production for their very own "weather channel," modeled on programs that they have seen on television. Groups could present information about the accuracy of local weather forecasts over the course of the project, their own predictions of weather using traditional methods, or the tools that meteorologists use to predict the weather. Math skills may be integrated as children take measurements and present their information in the form of charts and graphs. Videotaping the various "shows" will result in a final product that the students can enjoy together as a class and that will serve as a model for future classes.

Resources for "Forecasting the Weather"

Stories:

Cloudy With a Chance of Meatballs by Judi Barrett, illustrated by Ron Barrett (Atheneum, 1978)

Geoffrey Groundhog Predicts the Weather by Bruce Koscielniak (Houghton Mifflin, 1995)

If Frogs Made the Weather by Marion Dane Bauer, illustrated by Dorothy Donohue (Holiday House, 2005)

"Mr. Frost" by Posy Simmonds in *Little Lit: Strange Stories for Strange Kids* edited by Art Spiegelman and Françoise Mouly (HarperCollins, 2001)

Think Cool Thoughts by Elizabeth Perry, illustrated by Linda Bronson (Clarion, 2005)

Information Books:

How Does the Sun Make Weather? by Judith Williams (Enslow Elementary, 2005)

It's Windy! by Julie Richards (Smart Apple Media, 2005)

Meteorologists by Sandra J. Christian (Bridgestone Books, 2002)

On the Same Day in March: A Tour of the World's Weather by Marilyn Singer, illustrated by Frane Lessac (HarperCollins, 2000)

Rain and Shine by Deborah Kespert and Sue Barraclough, illustrated by Fran Jordan (Two-Can, 2000)

Today's Weather Is . . .: A Book of Experiments by Lorraine Jean Hopping, illustrated by Meredith Johnson (Mondo, 2000)

Watching the Weather by Edana Eckart (Children's Press, 2004)

Watching the Weather by Miranda Ashwell and Andy Owen (Heinemann Library, 1999)

Weather by Alice K. Flanagan (Compass Point Books, 2000)

Weather by Jim Pipe (Stargazer Books, 2005)

Weather by Lorrie Mack (DK Publishing, 2004)

Weather by Sally Hewitt (Children's Press, 1999)

Weather Forecasting by Gail Gibbons (Aladdin Paperbacks, 1987)

Weather Forecasting by Terri Sievert (Capstone Press, 2005)

Weather Patterns by Monica Hughes (Heinemann Library, 2004)

Weather Wise by Rebecca Weber, illustrated by Anna-Maria Crum (Compass Point Books, 2003)

Weather Words and What They Mean by Gail Gibbons (Holiday House, 1990)

What Makes Weather? by Helen Orme (Gareth Stevens, 2004)

What Will the Weather Be? by Lynda Dewitt, illustrated by Carolyn Croll (HarperCollins, 1991)

Whatever the Weather by Karen Wallace, illustrated by Gill Tomblin (DK Publishing, 1999)

What's the Weather Today? by Allan Fowler (Children's Press, 1991)

What's the Weather? by Melissa Stewart (Compass Point Books, 2005)

Videos and DVDs:

Investigating Weather [videorecording] by John Colgren (United Learning, 1995, 18 min.)

Weather: A First Look [videorecording] by Peter Cochran (Rainbow Educational Video, 2000, 18 min.)

Weather and Climate [videorecording] by Ronald C. Meyer (SVE & Churchill Media, 1999, 12 min.)

Weather: Changes and Measurement [videorecording] (100% Educational Videos, 1999)

Database searches and pre-selected Web sites if necessary.

PROJECT THREE: *Recycling*

Relevance

Recycling is a topic that all children are familiar with because schools and communities everywhere have recycling bins for plastic, metal, glass, and paper. Students like to show off their knowledge about how to recycle and why it is important. But they have probably never seen the process completed at recycling plants.

Discussion

Stories such as *Joseph Had a Little Overcoat* and *A Box Can Be Many Things* can get children thinking about common items that they themselves own that could be refashioned into useful objects. Ask the children to predict some new uses for the overcoat and the box before and during a dialogic reading. This can lead to making predictions about what they will see at a recycling plant. Sharing information books about recycling can make their research during library sessions and excursions meaningful and relevant. Once they visit a recycling plant, these sources can be examined again for comparison with the recycling operations in their own community.

Investigation

This investigation will demand hands-on work and direct observation, plus research using information sources. After a field trip, children will have many new questions. Some questions may arise that cannot be answered in the nonfiction sources. Mediated Internet searches to find statistics may be necessary.

End Product

The children will have lots of suggestions for possible end products. Perhaps they would like to produce a documentary about the life cycle of a bottle or pop can. Useful objects can be made from recycled materials. Items made from recycled material can be identified, both in the classroom and at home. Children may decide to share their new knowledge through an informative poster for the school. A poster might trace what happens to the items they recycle at the school and give relevant statistics about the school's recycling efforts. It could become an official document of the school as a poster or as part of the school's Web site. Videos, posters, pamphlets, and checklists are all appropriate formats with which to inform their classmates at school about the importance of recycling.

Resources for "Recycling"

Stories:

A Box Can Be Many Things by Dana Meachen Rau, illustrated by Paige Billin-Frye
(Children's Press, 1997)

Happy Dog Sizzles! by Lisa Grubb (Philomel, 2004)

Joseph Had a Little Overcoat by Simms Taback (Viking, 1999)

Recycled! by Jillian Powell, illustrated by Amanda Wood (Picture Window Books, 2000)

Recycle Every Day! by Nancy Elizabeth Wallace (Marshall Cavendish, 2003)

The Great Trash Bash by Loreen Leedy (Holiday House, 1991)

Information Books:

All New Crafts for Earth Day by Kathy Ross (Milbrook Press, 2006)

Earth Day – Hooray! by Stuart J. Murphy, illustrated by Renee Andriani (HarperCollins, 2004)

Earth Friends at Home by Francine Galko (Heinemann Library, 2004)

Earth Friends at Play by Francine Galko (Heinemann Library, 2004)

Earth Friends at School by Francine Galko (Heinemann Library, 2004)

Earth Friends at the Grocery Store by Francine Galko (Heinemann Library, 2004)

EcoArt!: Earth-Friendly Art & Craft Experiences for 3- to 9-Year-Olds by Laurie Carlson, illustrated by Loretta Trezzo Braren (Williamson, 1993)

Glass by Mary Firestone (Capstone Press, 2005)

I Drive a Garbage Truck by Sarah Bridges, illustrated by Derrick Alderman & Denise Shea (Picture Window, 2005)

Let's Recycle by Claire Llewellyn, illustrated by Paul B. Davies (Chrysalis Education, 2003)

Metal by Chris Oxlade (Heinemann Library, 2001)

Metal by Sara Louise Kras (Capstone Press, 2004)

Our Environment by Malcolm Penny (Raintree Steck-Vaughn, 2000)

Paper by Chris Oxlade (Heinemann Library, 2001)

Paper by Sara Louise Kras (Capstone Press, 2004)

Plastic by Chris Oxlade (Heinemann Library, 2001)

Plastic by Rhonda Donald Lucas (Capstone Press, 2004)

Rubber by Mary Firestone (Capstone Press, 2005)

Toil in the Soil by Michelle Myers Lackner, illustrated by Daniel Powers (Millbrook Press, 2001)

Too Much Trash! by Fay Robinson (Children's Press, 1995)

Waste Not: Time to Recycle by Rebecca Weber (Compass Point Books, 2003)

Where Does the Garbage Go? by Paul Showers, illustrated by Randy Chewning (HarperCollins, 1994)

Why Should I Recycle? by Jen Green, illustrated by Mike Gordon (Barron's, 2002)

Your Environment by Brenda Williams (Raintree Steck-Vaughn, 1999)

Video:

Big Machines: Two ("Part 3: Where the Garbage Goes") [videorecording] by Fred Levine (Fred Levine Productions, 2003, 106 min.)

Garbage Day! [videorecording] produced by Mark Horowitz & William Schreiner (Childvision Educational Films, 1994, 23 min.)

Joseph Had a Little Overcoat [videorecording] directed and animated by Daniel Ivanick (Weston Woods, 2001, 10 min.)

Keeping Your Community Clean [videorecording] by David Creech (Rainbow Educational Media, 1995, 16 min.)

My First Green Video: A Kid's Guide to Ecology and Environmental Activities [videorecording] by Angela Wilkes (Sony Kids' Video, 1993, 43 min.)

Taking Care of Our Earth [videorecording] by Allison Piccolo, Colleen Jackson, and Karen Olson (100% Educational Videos, 1999, 16 min.)

PROJECT FOUR: *Our Favorite Information Books*

 ## Relevance

Information sources themselves can be the subject of an investigation through the project approach. Just as children at this age explore stories and writers because of the pleasure they bring, so too they can look at information books as worthy of pursuit for their interest value alone. A well-stocked library should have at least one information book that a child would choose for pleasure reading. If this is the case, a project focusing on informational books themselves is possible.

Free voluntary reading of nonfiction is just as important as fiction. An examination of their reading tastes in information books will raise awareness of the riches that are out there in the nonfiction section of the library. Because the ultimate subject of the project is chosen by each student, it will be relevant and engaging.

 ## Discussion

A fun way to introduce a project on nonfiction reading is to have the children list all of the nonfiction topics that they can. Children should be asked to write down their own personal favorites before they go to the library, though they are free to change their minds if they happen upon something more interesting while browsing the shelves. A secret ballot to predict which topics will be the most popular choices will add some suspense to the activity. The library media specialist and the teacher will be kept busy in the next library session as the children select a book that they will present as part of a project on "Our Favorite Information Books."

Human Dewey Chart

Once all of the children have found a book and they are happy with their choices, it is time to see where their interests lie. One concrete way of expressing this is through a "Human Dewey Chart." In a large open area, children can be asked to line up with their selection under the Dewey number that begins the number on the spine of their book. Thus, all the children who chose books about wild animals will be in the number five line, while those with books about Ancient Egypt or Roman armies will be at number nine. Once the lines are formed, the children can have a seat and begin their investigation into the reading interests of their class.

 ## Investigation

Students can take turns holding up their book and describing its contents. Then it is time for their observations. What do they note about the graph? Which line is longest? Why? Were some numbers not chosen at all? Why not? Does this make sense to them? What section of Dewey probably has the greatest number of books? Children will probably have some perceptive comments about the logic behind

Dewey as well. Often, children will gravitate to books about animals. Why is it that some of them are in the number six line and others are in the number five? The class will enjoy tackling these questions. The librarian will not need to teach them anything about Dewey directly – the children will figure it out for themselves. A good way to conclude this important opening discussion is to take an "aerial" shot of the Dewey chart so that students can consult it later in their class. It easily can be converted into a bar graph later on by the students.

▶ End Product

Children might want to work with others who have chosen similar topics or work on their own. Whatever they decide, collectively they can come up with questions and observations that will help them to explain their nonfiction reading choices to their colleagues. How are their books organized? Do they have special features such as diagrams or photographs? What about a bibliography or glossary at the back? How do they read the book? Flip through it first, looking at pictures? Choose a chapter with an interesting title? Read it from cover to cover? What makes the book appealing? Have they read similar books? How do they compare to this one? These questions and comments can be explored both in the classroom and the library as children decide how they will present their book in their end product.

The library media specialist can help to model nonfiction booktalks with a few favorite books of her own. Questions that remain about the Dewey Decimal System can be addressed. Why are certain subjects together? A discussion of nonfiction may also lead to questions that may never have occurred to them before, such as how the librarian makes nonfiction selections and if they can make requests for certain kinds of books. The librarian can share statistics about how many and what kinds of nonfiction books circulate. She might show them some reviewing tools that she uses to find good books for the collection. Children might choose to do a booktalk, write a book review, or demonstrate something that they have learned to do by reading a nonfiction book. All of these final products can be modeled by the librarian and then the evaluation criteria can be developed by the students and the teacher back in the classroom. The result will be a rich variety of models for children to view the following year.

Works Cited

American Association of School Librarians. *Information Power: Building Partnerships for Learning*. Chicago: American Library Association, 1998.

Arizona Department of Education. *Early Learning Standards*. Apr. 2005 <http://www.ade.az.gov/earlychildhood/downloads/EarlyLearningStandards.pdf>

Barnett, W. Steven, Kirsty Brown, and Rima Shore. "The Targeted vs. Universal Debate: Should the United States Have Preschool for All?" *Preschool Policy Matters* 6 Apr. 2004. 21 June 2005 <http://nieer.org/resources/policybriefs/6.pdf>

Bowman, Barbara T., M. Suzanne Donovan, and M. Susan Burns (Eds.). *Eager to Learn: Educating Our Preschoolers*. Washington, DC: National Academies Press.

Bredekamp, Sue (Ed.). *Developmentally Appropriate Practice in Early Childhood Programs Serving Children From Birth Through Age 8*. Washington, DC: NAEYC, 1987.

Bredekamp, Sue, and Carol Copple (Eds.). *Developmentally Appropriate Practice in Early Childhood Programs*. Washington, DC: NAEYC, 1997.

Cardman, Michael. "Researchers Argue for Universal Preschool Services." *Education Daily* 29 June 2004: 3.

Diffily, Deborah, and Charlotte Sassman. *Project-Based Learning with Young Children*. Portsmouth, NH: Heinemann, 2002.

Driscoll, Amy, and Nancy G. Nagel. *Early Childhood Education, Birth-8: The World of Children, Families, and Educators*. Boston: Pearson, 2005.

Elkind, David. "Piaget, Jean (1896-1980)." *The Encyclopedia of Education*. Ed. James W. Guthrie. 8 vols. New York: Thomson Gale, 2003.

Feiler, Rachelle, and Dana Tomonari. "Child Development, Stages of Growth." *The Encyclopedia of Education*. Ed. James W. Guthrie. 8 vols. New York: Thomson Gale, 2003.

Ferrandino, Vincent L., and Gerald N. Tirozzi. *Early Education Ensures That We Leave No Child Behind: Principals' Perspective*. 5 Sept. 2001. National Association of Elementary School Principals. 21 June 2005 <www.naesp.org/ContentLoad.do?contentId=891>

Georgia Department of Early Care and Learning. *Georgia's Pre-K Program Content Standards*. July 2005 (Revised) <http://www.decal.state.ga.us/Documents/PreK/Content_Standards_Full.pdf>

Gredler, Margaret E. "Vygotsky, Lev (1896-1934)." *The Encyclopedia of Education*. Ed. James W. Guthrie. 8 vols. New York: Thomson Gale, 2003.

Head Start Bureau. *Head Start Child Outcomes Framework*. 2001 <www.headstartinfo.org/pdf/im00_18a.pdf>

Helm, Judy Harris, and Lillian Katz. *Young Investigators: The Project Approach in the Early Years*. New York: Teachers College Press, 2001.

Hoyt, Linda. *Make It Real: Strategies for Success With Informational Texts*. Portsmouth, NH: Heinemann, 2002.

International Reading Association, and National Association for the Education of Young Children. *Learning to Read and Write: Developmentally Appropriate Practices for Young Children, pt. 1*. 22 June 2005 <www.naeyc.org/about/positions/psread1.asp>

Kagan, Sharon L., and Catherine Scott-Little. "Early Learning Standards: Changing the Parlance and Practice of Early Childhood Education?" *Phi Delta Kappan* 85.5 (Jan. 2004): 388-96.

Katz, Lillian G., and Sylvia C. Chard. *Engaging Children's Minds: The Project Approach*. Stamford: Ablex Publishing, 2000.

Kendall, John S. "Setting Standards in Early Childhood Education." *Educational Leadership* 60.7 (Apr. 2003): 64-8.

Kessenich, Maureen et al. "Developmental Theory." *The Encyclopedia of Education*. Ed. James W. Guthrie. 8 vols. New York: Thomson Gale, 2003.

Mallett, Margaret. *Early Years Non-Fiction: A Guide to Helping Young Researchers Use and Enjoy Information Texts*. London: RoutledgeFalmer.

Malley, Cathy. *Preschooler Development*. Ames, IA: NNCC, 2002 <www.nncc.org/Child.Dev/presch.dev.html>

Music & Songs: Garden. Preschool Education, 2005 <www.preschooleducation.com/sgarden.shtml>

National Association for the Education of Young Children. *Developmentally Appropriate Practice in Early Childhood Programs Serving Children from Birth through Age 8: A Position Statement of the National Association for the Education of Young Children*. Washington, DC: NAEYC, 1997 <www.naeyc.org/about/positions/pdf/PSDAP98.PDF>

National Association for the Education of Young Children. *Technology and Young Children – Ages 3 Through 8: A Position Statement of the National Association for the Education of Young Children*. Washington, DC: NAEYC, 1996 <www.naeyc.org/about/positions/pdf/PSTECH98.PDF>

National Association for the Education of Young Children, and National Association of Early Childhood Specialists in State Departments of Education. *Early Learning Standards: Creating the Conditions for Success*. Washington, DC: NAEYC, 2002 <www.naeyc.org/about/positions/pdf/position_statement.pdf>

National Research Council. *Eager to Learn: Educating Our Preschoolers*. Washington, DC: National Academy Press, 2001.

Oesterreich, Lesia. *Ages & Stages – Five-Year-Olds*. Ames, IA: NNCC, 2002 <www.nncc.org/Child.Dev/ages.stages.5y.html>

Oesterreich, Lesia. *Ages & Stages – Six- Through Eight-Year-Olds*. Ames, IA: NNCC, 2002 <www.nncc.org/Child.Dev/ages.stages.6y.8y.html>

Portalupi, Joann, and Ralph Fletcher. *Nonfiction Craft Lessons: Teaching Information Writing K-8*. Portland: Stenhouse Publishers, 2001.

"Preschool for All: Quality Care, Education for All Young Children." *Nation's Cities Weekly* 8 Feb. 2002: 8.

"Preschool for Everyone." *Time* 9 Nov. 1998: 98.

Sameroff, Karnold, and Susan C. McDonough. "Educational Implications of Developmental Transitions: Revisiting the 5- to 7-Year Shift." *Phi Delta Kappan* 76.3 (Nov. 1994): 200-5.

Scott-Little, Catherine, Sharon Lynn Kagan, and Victoria Stebbins Frelow. "Creating the Conditions for Success with Early Learning Standards: Results from a National Study of State-Level Standards for Children's Learning Prior to Kindergarten." *ECRP: Early Childhood Research and Practice* 5.2 (Fall 2003) <http://ecrp.uiuc.edu/v5n2/little.html>

Scott-Little, Catherine, Sharon Lynn Kagan, and Victoria Stebbins Frelow. *Inside the Content: The Breadth and Depth of Early Learning Standards*. Greensboro, NC: SERVE, March 2005 <http://www.serve.org/_downloads/publications/insidecontentes.pdf>

Shonkoff, Jack P., and Deborah A. Phillips. (Eds.). *From Neurons to Neighborhoods: The Science of Early Childhood Development*. Washington, DC: National Academy Press, 2000.

Stead, Tony. *Is That a Fact? Teaching Nonfiction Writing K-3*. Portland: Stenhouse Publishers, 2002.

Vygotsky, L. [Lev] S. *Mind in Society: The Development of Higher Psychological Processes*. Cambridge: Harvard University Press.

Walker, Carolyn, Sherry Kragler, Linda Martin, and Ashlee Arnett. "Facilitating the Use of Informational Texts in a 1st Grade Classroom." *Childhood Education* 79.3 (Spring 2003): 152(8). *Student Resource Center Gold*. GaleNet. 25 Mar. 2005 <www.galegroup.com>

Whitehurst, Grover J. *How to Read to Your Preschooler*. 1992 <http://caselinks.education.ucsb.edu/casetrainer/CLADContent/Cladlanguage/node4/practice/DialogicReading.htm>

Wilgoren, Jodi. "Union Leader Will Propose Total Access to Head Start." *The New York Times* 12 July 2001: A16.

Index

ELEPHANTS

Joyce Poole

Voyageur Press

Contents

Introduction

One morning in February 1989 I was out on the Amboseli plains with Jezebel's family. The adult females were in a sleepy mid-morning sort of mood. At their feet the youngsters played their favorite game, King of the Castle. A juvenile female lay on her side wriggling her large gray body and flopping her trunk about while several babies attempted to clamber on top of her. Joshua, Joyce's teenage son, was much too old for this juvenile game of wiggling, but still too young and energetic to feel sleepy, and he came over to see what I was doing instead. I was sitting on the hood of my car taking photographs and, as he approached, I rumbled softly to him. He raised his trunk high in the air, taking in all the scents that belonged to me, and came closer. I, too, was in the mood for a game. I took off one of my old rubber flip-flops and tossed it to him. He reached his trunk tentatively toward the shoe, relaxed and elongated it, hesitated, and then swung his trunk toward my shoe again, sniffing it over and over until he decided it was safe to touch. He stretched his trunk out to its full length and picked up the flip-flop. So began our game.

Joshua had not met a flip-flop before, and so it required detailed investigation involving prolonged contact with various parts of his body. He grasped it firmly with his trunk and first stabbed it with the tip of his tusk, and then used it to scratch the underside of his trunk, which made a lovely rasping sound against the ridges of thick elephant skin. Finally he put it in his mouth and carefully chewed it, turning it slowly over and over with his large tongue. After several minutes of such examination he tossed the shoe up in the air behind him. Listening carefully to where it fell, he opened and closed his eyes as if considering the interesting new sound that it had made and then, waggling his head in an indication of amusement, he reversed several steps and

A newborn calf is helped to its feet by its mother and other family members.

reached back to touch it gently with his hind foot. Having touched it carefully from all angles and with both hind feet, he stepped firmly on it, scuffed it through the dust, stepped on it again, and then, with his back legs crossed casually, he contemplated the flip-flop in deep elephant silence.

When we humans contemplate an object, we look at it intently. Elephants take it in sensually. Joshua stood quietly, facing away from the flip-flop, perhaps reliving the wonderful new feelings he had experienced. Then he reversed further, reached back with his trunk, picked up the flip-flop, and started the game all over again. Finally, he tossed my shoe, under-trunk, back toward me. I picked my shoe off the ground, found it undamaged, and threw it back to him. We did this a couple of times until something else caught my attention, and I looked away for a minute. The next thing I knew something hard landed on my head and fell to the ground with a thud. Joshua had found a small piece of wildebeest bone and had thrown it at me with surprising accuracy. Joshua, a wild elephant, had understood and was entertained by our game: there we were, two species out on the plains playing catch.

An Asian elephant uses its trunk as a snorkle.

Elephants are the earth's largest land mammal. Their massive size and extraordinary appearance are awe-inspiring. Those who have had a chance to watch their behavior in the wild are struck by their strong family bonds and by the tenderness with which elephants care for their young.

Elephants clear away floating vegetation before sucking water into their trunks.

This African elephant family consists of three adult females and six immature offspring. Young calves remain close to their mother's side and suckle until they are four or five years old. Families are characterized by close social bonds. Family members defend one another in times of danger and show strong affiliative behavior. Females will remain with their family for life, while males will depart at around 14 years old.

I have had the privilege of spending 14 years in Amboseli National Park in southern Kenya studying the sexual behavior and vocal communication of African elephants. Now (2001) in its 29th year, the Amboseli Elephant Research Project, directed by Cynthia Moss, is the longest and most detailed study of wild elephants anywhere in the world. The population's 1120 elephants are each known individually, and their family histories and relationships are recorded in detail. Along with my colleagues, I have had the unusual opportunity to know elephants as individuals with unique characters.

Elephants detect scents we cannot smell and voices we cannot hear.

It is not only their size that sets elephants apart from most other animals, but their social complexity, intelligence, range and intensity of expression, and their understanding of death. After all this time, I still find myself with so many unanswered questions about these amazing creatures. On many occasions I have watched the excited greeting ceremony of related elephants: massive bodies spinning around urinating and defecating, temporal glands streaming, and a cacophony of ear-splitting trumpets, roars, screams and rumbles. Each time I wonder whether this display is simply a message to other elephants that the family is, once more, a force to be reckoned with or whether the elephants are actually expressing their joy at being together again. I have witnessed the intense excitement displayed by elephants at the birth of a baby, as ten, perhaps 20 elephants vocalize in chorus, their calls extraordinarily powerful, some well below the level of human hearing, reaching over 106 decibels, and traveling 3 to 6 miles (5 to 10 km). These scenes are typical of elephants during moments of social excitement; a greeting, a birth, a mating, for example. What is the function of this phenomenal chorus of calls? Are specific messages being transmitted to other elephants, or are they, as humans would be, simply overcome by the excitement of the occasion?

I have watched a female elephant die and observed other elephants spend close to an hour trying to raise her. And I have witnessed, two days later, the same elephants return to visit her butchered carcass. They stood in ghastly silence as they touched repeatedly her bloodied face where her tusks had been removed with an axe. Why did they come back? What thoughts, if any, did they have? I have observed a mother, her facial expression one I could recognize as grief, stand beside her stillborn baby for three days, and I have been moved deeply by the eerie silence of an elephant family as, for an hour, they fondled the bones of their matriarch. What were these elephants actually feeling? Was their 'grief', their 'mourning' in any way similar to our own?

I have played silly trumpeting games with young wild elephants and they have shown, by their facial expressions, that they remembered our game over two years later. What were they thinking as they walked past my car, waggling their heads and ears at me, their mouths pulled back in what appeared to be a 'smile'? I have had elephants gather in calm silence around my car to listen to my singing. Did they enjoy the melody? Whatever the answers to these questions, I am sure that the more we learn about elephants the fainter the line we have drawn between man and other animals will become. But time is running out for the elephants. If we can't find a way to accommodate one of the earth's most magnificent creatures, what possible hope is there for the myriad other less significant animals? What hope is there for us?

Elephants have favorite scratching trees and the bark is worn smooth from years of use.

Origins

Elephants belong to the larger group or order of mammals called the Proboscidea, so named after their most notable organ – the proboscis, or trunk. The Proboscideans include 354 recognized species of which 351 are now extinct; the African savannah elephant, *Loxodonta africana*, the African forest elephant, *Loxodonta cyclotis*, and the Asian elephant, *Elephas maximus*, are the sole survivors of an extensive radiation which began their differentiation over 60 million years ago.

Recent molecular evidence indicates that the Proboscidea belong in a newly recognized super order, Afrotheria. In addition to elephants, Afrotheria includes hyraxes, sea cows, aardvarks, golden moles, tenrecs and elephant shrews, each of which originated in Africa. A distinct subgroup, Paenungulata, links elephants, hyraxes and sea cows. The Proboscideans' long and spectacular evolutionary history probably originated in North Africa with a creature named *Phosphatherium esculliei,* which lived in the late Cretaceous some 62 million years ago in what is present-day Morocco. *Phosphatherium* was about the size of a dog and, lacking a trunk, did not look anything like a modern elephant. Its teeth, however, were distinctly elephantine and looked almost identical to the next closest elephant forebear, *Moeritherium lyonsi*. *Moeritherium* was a small, aquatic, pig-sized creature, which possessed neither tusks nor trunk, although both its upper and lower jaws contained elongated teeth. This elephant ancestor lived in north-east Africa during the early Eocene epoch, and into the Oligocene epoch, about 50–35 million years ago.

Also living in north-east Africa some 40 million years ago were *Palaeomastodon* and *Phiomia*, large mammals which possessed tusks in both the upper and lower jaws. Their most distinctive features were strong and

Elephants use their excellent spatial memory to locate water in the arid Namibian Bush.

elongated lips and jaws which enabled them to feed by grasping leaves and grasses. *Palaeomastodon*, in particular, showed the closest beginnings of a trunk, and stood about 6.5 ft (2 m) at the shoulder. It is likely that these four mammals, *Phosphatherium, Moeritherium, Palaeomastodon* and *Phiomia*, made up the basic stock from which all other elephant-like creatures evolved.

By the Miocene, some 35 million years ago, a host of Proboscideans had radiated from Africa to Europe, Asia and North America, and among them were the deinotheres. *Deinotherium* ('terrible beast') was a massive animal, almost the size of contemporary elephants, with large tusks which came from the lower jaw and turned sharply downward so that their tips faced almost backward. It has been surmised that these were used for raking submerged vegetation from the bottom of swamps. The highly successful deinotheres survived until comparatively recently, becoming extinct only 2–3 million years ago.

Another very successful group of Proboscideans included the gomphotheres and their allies, a widespread group whose remains have been discovered in Miocene deposits in Africa, Asia, Europe and North America. The Gomphotheriidae were nearly as large as an Asian elephant with two pairs of tusks, one pair in the upper jaw and one in the lower jaw. Based on the position of the external nasal opening, the short neck and long limbs, it is speculated that *Gomphotherium* had a well developed trunk.

The family Elephantidae began with *Stegotetrabelodon* and *Stegodibelodon,* primitive forms restricted to Africa in the late Miocene and early Pliocene. These two genera lived in a mixed forest and savannah environment. Although they were similar to modern elephants in a host of ways, there were some important differences relating to the shape of their teeth, and the presence of incisors in the lower jaw.

Stegotetrabelodon gave rise to *Primelephas* which lived in open wooded savannah in east and central Africa about 6–7 million years ago. *Primelephas* stood as tall as a female African elephant and had two pairs of tusks protruding

Asian elephants are more closely related to the
extinct mammoths than they are to African elephants.

African and Asian elephants may be distinguished easily. African elephants are the larger species; they have bigger ears and a concave-shaped back. Asian elephants have smaller ears, a convex-shaped back and a large domed forehead.

forward, the upper pair over 3 ft (1 m) long, and the lower pair much shorter. *Primelephas* became the basic stock for three genera of elephants. First was the rather primitive *Loxodonta* which contains two species, one of which survives today as the African elephant. A second branch was the more progressive *Elephas,* including 11 species of which only one survives today as the Asian elephant. A third branch contained the mammoths, genus *Mammuthus.*

Fossil mammoth remains have been found in Africa, Eurasia, and North America. Perhaps the best known member of this genus was the woolly mammoth, *Mammuthus primigenius,* which survived until the very end of the Ice Age in the far northern hemisphere. The mammoth was contemporary with modern humans and numerous paintings have been found of this species in caves in Europe. In addition, frozen well-preserved carcasses have been found in Siberia and Alaska, which provide extraordinary detail of the anatomy of these creatures. Their bodies were covered with long hair and dense underwool and their tusks were long, curving first outward and then inward.

These Proboscideans, *Stegodibelodon, Stegotetrabelodon, Primelephas, Loxodonta, Elephas*, and *Mammuthus,* together make up the family Elephantidae. All members of the family, living and extinct, possess a well developed trunk. Fossil specimens of Elephantidae have been found in Africa, Europe, Asia, North America and Central America.

The two African elephants, *Loxodonta africana, Loxodonta cyclotis,* and the Asian elephant, *Elephas maximus,* are the only living representatives of the family. In prehistoric times, *Loxodonta* was found throughout the African continent, but never beyond, while *maximus* originated in Africa and then migrated to Europe and Asia.

The most obvious superficial difference between African and Asian elephants is the size of the ears: African elephants have very large ears while Asian elephants have smaller ears. People enjoy pointing out that the ear of an African elephant is shaped like the continent of Africa, while the Asian elephant's ear is shaped like the Indian sub continent. Another obvious difference is the shape of the back: an African elephant's is concave in shape, while the Asian elephant's is convex, hence its name, *Elephas maximus*, or huge arch ('ele' from the Greek meaning arch, 'phant' meaning huge, and 'maximus' meaning large from the Latin *maxima*). The highest point of an African elephant is its shoulder, while the Asian elephant's highest point is the top of its head, which, unlike its cousin's, is twin-domed. African elephants are significantly less hairy than Asian elephants, probably because the latter is more closely related to the woolly mammoth. African elephants have two finger-like tips at the end of their trunk, while the Asian elephant has only one. Another less obvious difference to the casual observer is the shape of the chewing surfaces of the teeth. The tooth plates of African elephants are composed of lozenge-shaped enamel loops, hence the genus name, *Loxodonta*, 'lox' meaning lozenge and 'odon' referring to tooth. The plates on a tooth of an Asian elephant, however, are closed compressed loops.

The Asian elephant includes three subspecies, *Elephas maximus maximus* found on Sri Lanka, *Elephas maximus indicus* in peninsular India and throughout South-east Asia, and *Elephas maximus sumatranus*, the smallest of the three, on Sumatra. Recent genetic data suggest the designation of a fourth subspecies from Borneo, *Elephas maximus borneensis*.

In Africa, two species, the savannah (*Loxodonta africana*) and forest (*Loxodonta cyclotis*) elephant, are now generally recognized and a third West African species has been proposed. The better-known savannah elephant ranges widely in the grassland and bush country of east-central and southern Africa and has large ears and curving tusks. The less commonly seen African forest elephant lives in densely forested areas of central Africa and is slightly smaller, has rounded ears and straighter, downward-pointing tusks.

An Asian elephant tosses dust over his back.

The Largest of Land Mammals

African and Asian elephants share a long list of traits that are unusual among mammals, the most obvious being the possession of a trunk, a massive body, large ears, elongated incisors made of ivory, and thick skin (hence the term 'pachyderm'). Other characteristics shared by all species include their sparsely distributed body hair, the location of the external genitalia of both males and females between the hind legs, the lungs attached to the diaphragm, a heart with a double-pointed apex (instead of a typical one-point mammalian heart), two anterior vena cavae, the lack of a gall bladder, and the testes located inside the abdomen near the kidneys. The elephants are different in so many respects from other mammals that a review of their anatomy and physiology is fascinating.

Elephants are the largest living land mammals and sexual dimorphism (morphological differences between males and females) in body size is extreme. Females begin approaching a plateau in height and weight growth in their late twenties, while males continue to grow through most of their lives, eventually reaching twice the weight of adult females. Male African savannah elephants may attain a weight of over 13,000 lb (6000 kg) while females reach only half that weight. By the time a male elephant reaches sexual maturity, at about 17 years old, his shoulder height exceeds that of a fully grown female. Yet at this size he is still a mere teenager. He is only 80% of his full adult height and a little over half his full adult weight; he cannot begin to compete with older males for mates. Unlike most other mammals, elephants continue to grow in body size long after puberty. The ability of elephants to continue growing in height beyond the age of sexual maturity is related to the unusual delayed epiphyseal fusion of the long bones, a pattern more pronounced in males than in females. The epiphyses are a part of the bone that ossifies separately from the

Elephants are gray, but mud comes in many colors.

23

main part of the bone, and until they have fused and ossified, reflect continued growth. Among female elephants, fusion of the epiphyses occurs around 25 years of age, whereas in males epiphyseal fusion takes place between the ages of 35 and 45. There has undoubtedly been strong selective pressure for large body size in male elephants.

Over the course of the elephants' long evolutionary history, the trend has been for increasing body size. As the Proboscideans became larger, they required stronger support for their increasing weight. The result was the evolution of legs positioned almost vertically under the body (similar to the legs of a table), rather than the angular position of most other mammals. These pillar-like legs provide strong support for their massive weight, and an elephant can doze in a standing position for long periods without expending much energy. Unlike other mammals, however, an elephant must keep at least one foot on the ground at all times. Thus an elephant cannot trot, canter, gallop or jump. An elephant's normal walking speed is about 4 mph (6 kph), but a shuffling run of up to 16 mph (25 kph) may be attained. Compared to other animals, elephants spend a surprising amount of time walking backwards. This is because turning around requires a 'three-point-turn', and backing up for short distances uses less energy. Elephants cover an average of 15 miles (25 km) a day, but they can easily walk over 45 miles (70 km). In the desert of Namibia movements of up to 120 miles (195 km) in a day have been recorded.

Elephants are said to be the best swimmers among land dwelling mammals and they obviously enjoy playing in the water. Whole groups of elephants may gather in deep water simply to play. An elephant may disappear underwater with only the tip of its trunk, used as a snorkle, showing above the surface, and then suddenly breach like a whale, flopping on its side with a great splash. Elephants have been seen completely upside-down with only the soles of their four feet showing above the water. Babies can swim almost as soon as

*Elephants walk on the tips of their fingers and toes. Inside each foot,
the digits rise to meet the wrist or heel bones. These rest on a fibrous pad, inside the
foot, which acts as a shock-absorber for the elephant's enormous weight.*

A cooling mud wallow is a favorite activity for a hot day.
Vigorous kicking with the front legs and careful aim with trunkfulls of mud
can cover most of the body with mud. Sometimes simply lying down works best
and even a fully grown adult male enjoys a good wiggle in the mud.

they can walk and have been observed suckling underwater, leaving only the tip of their trunk above the surface to breathe.

The skin of an elephant may be as thick as 1 in (2.5 cm) or more on its back, head and the soles of its feet, while the skin on the posterior side of the ear, around the mouth and the anus, is paper-thin. Despite its thick, rough and bumpy appearance, the skin of an elephant is an extremely sensitive organ. For example, elephants frequently use the soles of their hind feet to examine objects or gently to wake up small calves.

The skin of both African and Asian elephants is lighter or darker gray in color (although some elephants are dappled with pink due to a genetic lack of pigmentation) and the range of tan, chocolate brown to ochre-colored elephants is merely a consequence of wallowing and dusting in different colored soils. Mud wallowing and dusting not only feels good but helps to protect the skin against ultraviolet radiation, insect bites and moisture loss.

One of the characteristics of modern elephants is that they have very little body hair. Sparse hair and bristles are distributed unevenly over the body, concentrated around eyes, ear openings, the chin, the trunk, and the end of the tail. The hair on the trunk, in particular, is associated with nerve endings which provide discriminatory tactile sensations.

The skin of an elephant is rough and fissured.

In comparison to other mammals elephants have a small surface area to body weight ratio, and therefore they cannot dissipate heat energy as readily. To solve the potential problem of over-heating elephants are anatomically adapted with large ears which function as heat radiators. The skin on the back side of the ears is only some $\frac{1}{10}$ in (2 mm) thick and is supplied with numerous blood vessels. By flapping their ears rhythmically back and forth, elephants are able to cool the circulating blood and therefore control their body temperature.

An elephant's ears also have numerous communication functions. Large, widely spaced ears are perfectly designed for listening in to distant, low-frequency sound waves, like those produced by calling elephants. And when elephants are vocalizing they typically flap their ears rapidly. The position of the ear, the type of movement, and the rate of flapping appear to be specific to the kind of call being produced, and by raising and flapping their ears elephants may be able to affect subtly the quality of the sound. Ear flapping is most vigorous during periods of social excitement when, among African elephants, secretion from the temporal glands is most noticeable. Ear flapping may also waft the odor from the temporal glands, located behind the eyes, which is used in olfactory communication, toward other elephants.

In Asian elephants rapid ear flapping may indicate aggression or agitation, while in African elephants similar posturing is an indication of social excitement. Among African elephants ear spreading, ear waving and ear folding may be part of an elephant's threat repertoire, and other elephants (and humans) ignore these messages at their peril. A silent charge with ears folded, trunk curled under, and head down is far more serious than the Hollywood mock charge typified by loud trumpets, head and tusks high, ears extended, and trunk outstretched. On the other hand, an ear fold associated with ears raised high, loud screaming, trumpeting and rumbling, though initially terrifying, is merely an elephant's greeting ceremony. Just as young elephants must learn to read ear language, so anyone who works with elephants must learn to understand their signals.

In their lifetime Asian and African elephants have 26 teeth which include

Elephants' eyes, small but wise, are the color of old amber.

two upper incisors, the tusks, 12 deciduous premolars and 12 molars. Once again elephants are an exception, as they do not replace teeth in a vertical manner (i.e. from above or below) as most mammals do, but rather in a horizontal progression. A newborn elephant has two to three teeth in each quadrant and, as it ages, new, bigger teeth develop from behind, slowly moving forward to replace these. As these bigger teeth come into wear they continue to move forward, eventually fragmenting, bit by bit, at the anterior edge and falling out of the mouth, or being swallowed. The timing and rate of tooth replacement is similar for both elephant species. The first teeth are replaced at 2–3 years old, the second at 4–6 years, the third at 12–15 years, the fourth at around 25–30 years and the fifth at 40–45. The sixth molar comes into full wear at about 43 years old and must last the elephant for the rest of its life.

Elephant tusks are composed mostly of dentine and, in cross-section, exhibit a unique pattern of lines that criss-cross one another in a zigzag or diamond shaped pattern. It is this pattern that makes elephant ivory unique. Elephants are born with deciduous incisors, or milk tusks, and these are replaced by permanent tusks within 6–12 months of birth. In African elephants these small growing tusks first show beyond the elephant's lip at approximately 18 months for males and closer to two years for females. Tusks then grow continuously at a rate of approximately 7 in (17 cm) per year, though the tusks of male African elephants apparently grow even faster late in life.

Typically, only two-thirds of the tusk is visible, the rest being embedded in the socket within the cranium. An elephant's tusks, as with all mammalian teeth, have pulp cavities containing highly vascularized tissues innervated by fine nerve branches making them sensitive to external pressure.

Both male and female African elephants carry tusks, although the rate of tusklessness is always higher among females. The degree of tusklessness among

Tusks are a useful resting place for a 300 lb (136 kg) nose.

females varies from one population to the next, from less than 2% to 15% or more. To a large extent tusklessness reflects the degree of ivory exploitation the population has undergone. In heavily poached populations where hunters select tusked elephants, as many as 40% of the large adult females are tuskless. Since tusklessness is hereditary, these populations have witnessed an increasing proportion of tuskless young elephants in recent years. Among Asian elephants the tusks of females are vestigial (present in the socket, but not visible below the lip) or totally absent, and tuskless males, known as 'mukhna', are much more common. The tusks of Asian elephants are considerably shorter and lighter than those of African elephants. The longest recorded tusks for an African elephant measured 10.7 ft (3.26 m), and the heaviest weighed 226.4 lb (102.7 kg). By comparison the record length for an Asian elephant is 9.9 ft (3.02 m) and the record weight only 86 lb (39 kg).

Males in full musth secrete a viscous liquid from enlarged temporal glands, located behind the eyes, and leave a trail of strong-smelling urine. High ranking males lose as much as 63 gal (240 liters) of urine in 24 hours.

Among African elephants there is strong sexual dimorphism in tusk weight. The tusks of males grow exponentially with age, and by 55 years old the tusks of males are seven times the weight of the tusks of females. The average tusk weight of a 55-year-old male is 108 lb (49 kg) per tusk, while the average tusk weight of a female of the same age is a mere 15 lb (7 kg) per tusk. It is the very much larger tusks of males that have made them so

Jezebel, a famous matriarch with long, asymmetrical tusks,
leads her family across Kenya's Amboseli plains.

Elephants are highly social animals; here Asian elephants gather in a forest habitat for the act of dusting.

vulnerable to ivory poachers. In many populations of elephants in Africa mature males are subject to elevated levels of poaching, making the sex ratio of breeding adults highly skewed toward females. The much thicker tusks of mature males creates an 'hour-glass' shaped face (broad foreheads, narrowing below the eyes and widening again at the tusk sockets), and this feature, in combination with the relatively larger heads of males, clearly distinguishes the two sexes at a glance.

Tusks are multipurpose instruments and are used by elephants to dig for water, minerals, and roots. They are very useful for prying bark off trees, breaking branches, or as levers for maneuvering felled trees. Elephants typically favor a particular tusk when handling food and years of use produces a deep groove which eventually breaks off. Tusks are important for both sexes in display and defense, and they are a matter of life and death for battling males. Domesticated elephants use their tusks for work, and all elephants with tusks use them as trunk rests.

It is the elephant's trunk that makes the Proboscidea truly unique. A fusion of the nose and the upper lip, the trunk has at its tip two openings which are, of course, the nostrils. But an elephant's trunk has far more uses than merely breathing. It is a highly sensitive organ equipped with an estimated 150,000 muscle units. At once a terrifically strong, and yet highly tactile and sensitive appendage, an elephant's trunk is, in many ways, more versatile than a human hand. It is used by elephants to eat and drink, to mudsplash and dust, to comfort and reassure, to lift and push, to fight and play, to attack and defend, to smell and vocalize. An elephant's trunk is, quite simply, indispensable. With this extraordinary number of uses it is hard to comprehend why such an appendage has not evolved in more than just the Proboscidea.

Using its trunk an elephant can push over a tree or pick up an object $\frac{1}{10}$ in (2 mm) in diameter. By flicking the tip of its trunk gently back and forth in a pool of water an elephant cleans dirt and floating vegetation away before drinking. By sucking water into its trunk an elephant can pour some 16 pints (9 liters) of water into its mouth at a time. An elephant is able to cover almost its entire body in a cooling mud bath, by careful aim of a trunkful of mud. By blowing through its trunk as it tosses dust on itself, an elephant is able to spread the powder evenly.

An elephant uses its trunk to rub itchy eyes or ears. And if the inside of its trunk has an itch, an elephant places the bothersome nostril over the tip of a tusk and twists it back and forth. A female elephant uses her trunk to reach back and touch a suckling baby, to calm one that is frightened or to pull one out of harm's way. An elephant greets a non-relative by placing its trunk in the other's mouth. An elephant uses its trunk to smell danger, to detect a female in estrus from several miles away, to track a rival male, and to recognize the urine or temporal gland secretion of members of its own family. By holding its trunk in different positions an elephant communicates with others, and by blowing through its trunk an elephant can produce a variety of different trumpets and snorts.

In the study of elephant behavior the position of an elephant's trunk is highly informative. The tip of the trunk is almost never stationary, moving in whatever direction the elephant finds interesting. An elephant's attention is usually stimulated by what other elephants are doing, and observing the trunk tip is a clue to both subtle behavior that is occurring or an interaction that is about to take place. An elephant's trunk and tusks are its most useful tools and many an elephant has learned that tusks do not conduct electricity and can be used to break electric fence wires. Elephants have been known intentionally to throw or drop large rocks and logs on the live wires of electric fences, either breaking the wire or loosening it so that it makes contact with the earth wire, thus shorting the fence.

Some tusks lend themselves for draping a trunk, others for tucking.

Elephants also use tools that they find in their environment. Elephants will hold a stick in their trunk and use it to remove a tick from between their forelegs. They may pick up a palm frond or similar piece of vegetation and use it as a fly swat to reach a part of the body that the trunk cannot. Elephants may pick up objects in their environments and throw them, under trunk, at their enemies or playmates with surprising accuracy.

Elephants are considered among the more intelligent of non-human animals. Perhaps, as in humans where the development of the brain paralleled the evolution of upright posture and the freeing of a dextrous hand for tool use, the complexity of an elephant's brain may be related to the use of its trunk.

Although the elephant's brain is small relative to its body size, weighing between 9 and 13 lb (4 and 6 kg), the cerebrum and cerebellum are highly convoluted. The temporal lobes of the cerebrum, which in humans function as the memory storage area, are very large, bulging out from the sides of the brain. Another measure of intelligence is the size of the brain at birth relative to its full adult size, which is considered to be an indication of the degree of learning a species undergoes during childhood. Among the majority of mammals this value is close to 90%. In humans the brain at birth is a mere 28% of its full adult size which, it has been argued, partly reflects the mechanical constraints of birth, but also indicates the long period of learning and social development that we undergo. Chimpanzees, our closest relatives, are born with 54% of their adult brain size. Elephants, too, are strikingly different from the majority of mammals with their brains at birth being only 35% of their full adult size, which in part must reflect the long period of dependency (about ten years) and learning (over 17 years) that young elephants go through. Intelligence is very difficult to measure, especially in a species whose senses are so different from our own, but certainly elephants are intelligent by non-human standards.

The Search for Food

An elephant's wide, flat teeth are perfectly designed for grinding the coarse plant material that makes up a large portion of its diet. Elephants feed in bulk, and, unlike ruminant herbivores such as buffaloes or antelopes, their fermentation chamber is in the hindgut (an enlarged caecum and colon) which is fairly inefficient at digesting plant fibre. Feeding may occupy from 60% to 70% of an elephant's waking hours; in the process of selective feeding an adult male may consume around 310 lb (140 kg) of wet forage in an average 24 hour period. An adult elephant may drink as much as 50 gallons (225 liters) of water a day. They can go without water for up to four days, but will drink several times a day if water is available.

Elephants eat grass, reeds, shrubs, herbs, creepers, trees, leaves, twigs, shoots, branches, thorns, succulent plants, bark, flowers, fruit pods, seeds, roots, and tubers. Each species of plant is handled in a specific way by using a variety of complex trunk, mouth, tusk, and foot movements. For example, with the two separate lobes or fingers on the end of its trunk, an African elephant can pluck individual leaves, flowers, or fruits from plants. Elephants can strip bunches of leaves from a branch, pull up a clump of grass, pick up fallen fruit from the ground, and can dig up roots, stolons, bulbs and tubers with sharp-edged toenails, trunk and tusks working together.

In general, elephants prefer high-quality grasses to woody plants because they have fewer chemical defenses and are easier to digest. Browse is, however, extremely important for nutritional balance. In open rangeland elephants feed mostly on grass during the wet season, when it is of high quality and in plentiful supply, and turn increasingly to browse as the dry season progresses. The diet of elephants living in woodlands and forests

A mature male has a deep scratch on a favorite rubbing tree.

contains more browse, but many studies have shown that grass is often taken in a higher proportion than its availability. Elephants living in forests feed extensively on fruit and, hence, are important seed dispersers.

With their enormous appetites and ability to consume almost all parts of the plants in their habitats, elephants have an almost unique potential, perhaps second only to man, for modifying their own environment dramatically over relatively short time scales. The changes in habitat caused by densities of elephants can affect other species, in extreme cases causing local extinction. Habitat change may even affect the elephants themselves, and when the food supply becomes depleted, they may move on or suffer reproductive failure or higher mortality. When elephants disappear from a savannah environment, the consequences may be marked and significant; places that were once grasslands supporting large populations of plains grazers and their predators become dense thickets with a lower biomass of predominantly browsing antelopes.

In many parts of Africa, the elephants have congregated in parks and reserves to avoid human encroachment and ivory poaching and this has led to conspicuous transformations in habitats. In such cases, wildlife managers may wish to take action to arrest these changes, such as manipulating water supplies and elephant distributions, fencing off patches of woodland, moving elephants elsewhere or simply shooting them to reduce local density. However, tropical environments are very dynamic and resilient in the face of disturbance. Woodlands may come and go, and come back yet again, in cycles which are regular or erratic and may take decades to unfold. It is important to take a large-scale perspective when we look at the balance between the state of the environment and the largest of land animals, and to harness both our imagination and our compassion when deciding what, if anything, needs to be done.

Elephants occupy a keystone position in the community of herbivores.

The Lives of the Two Sexes

Elephant social organization is usually described as being matriarchal, that is, a society in which families are led by females. While this is true, the label ignores male society, and theirs is equally fascinating. Perhaps the most fundamental behavioral difference between male and female elephants is that adult females and their dependent offspring live in tight-knit stable family groups, while adult males live more solitary, independent lives with few social bonds. Let us start where each elephant begins its life, with the family unit.

An elephant family is typically composed of several related females and their offspring. A family may be as small as two individuals, a mother and her calf, or as large as 40 or more individuals, including great-grandmothers, their daughters, their granddaughters, their great-granddaughters and their immature sons. Usually the oldest and largest adult female assumes the role of matriarch, and her leadership is both dramatic and pivotal when the family or an individual member faces danger or is in crisis. Contrary, however, to conventional wisdom, all adults participate in mundane decision making through a process of suggestion, negotation and consensus. The matriarch's role is gained through respect, not through force, and her extraordinary role of defender, reconciler and leader is obvious in the subtle deference of family members to her authority and her wishes. The bonds of the family radiate around her, and her death may cause a family to split up.

The size of an elephant family depends on many factors, but generally, families tend to be smaller in forest, woodland or bushland habitats, and larger in grassland ecosystems. This is because in grasslands individuals can remain in large close-knit groups and still obtain enough food, whereas in forests the habitat requires an individual to be more selective and thus inter-individual

With mouth wide open and ears flapping a mother calls to a member of her family.

distance must be greater. Within each of these habitats, however, larger and smaller families will occur, and the size of families is influenced by both the reproductive and survival success of individuals within the family as well as the strength of the friendships between the adult females.

There are many benefits associated with belonging to a large family. Larger families with older matriarchs tend to be dominant to smaller families with younger matriarchs, and are thus able to compete more successfully for scarce resources. Calves born into large families with more female caretakers are more likely to survive than calves born into smaller families.

Belonging to a large family is not the only way to obtain some of these benefits because the bonds of a female elephant extend out beyond the family in a series of multi-tiered relationships, through bond groups and clans. Bond groups are made up of one to five closely allied families that are usually related, and often result from the fission of family units. Above the level of the bond group is the clan, which has been defined as families that use the same dry season home range.

Elephants tend to aggregate during and immediately following the rainy seasons, when food is well distributed and plentiful. In African savannahs families may gather together in aggregations numbering several hundred individuals and over a thousand elephants have been observed in these wet-season gatherings. As the dry season progresses, the groups begin to split up. Apart from all the biological arguments that have been used to explain these congregations, such as breeding and survival benefits, it appears that elephants just plain enjoy being together, and will be if they can be. Interactions between females, both within and between families, are generally amicable except when there is competition over a scarce resource, such as food, water or minerals.

The size and structure of groups that a female elephant finds herself in depend upon a number of different social and environmental factors which include: the basic size of her family unit; the number of individuals making up

*Waterholes are important gathering places for elephants and the focus
of intense social behavior. As groups of elephants come and go, it is easy for a trained eye
to pick out the matriarch of each family and to discern which groups are related.*

During sexually inactive periods male elephants retire to bull areas where they interact in a relaxed and amiable manner. Males continue to grow through most of their lives and dominance is based on body size.

her bond group; the strength of bonds between her own and other families; the habitat type; the season; and, in many cases, the level of human threat.

Females become sexually mature and come into their first estrus anywhere from 8 to 18 years old depending on habitat quality and food availability. Gestation is an average 660 days long and females give birth to their first calf at anywhere from 10 to 20 years of age. Thereafter, depending upon food availability, females produce a calf on average every 4 to 6 years, slowing down as they approach 50 years old but often continuing into their sixties.

At birth, newborn elephants are welcomed into this tightly knit society by the loud roaring and rumbling of their older relatives. A pair of breasts, which look extraordinarily like those of a human female, are located between the mother's forelegs, more similar to the primates than to most other mammals. Newborns are able to stand within an hour and have their first suck of milk soon after. Young calves suck frequently (about every half hour for young males and every 50 minutes for females) and do not begin to feed on their own until they are around four months old. Calves continue to suckle until they are between four and six years old, and even eight-year-olds have been known to get down on their front wrists for a drink of milk. Typically calves are weaned, amidst very loud protests, when their mother is in late pregnancy with her next calf.

Techniques such as drinking, feeding, mudsplashing, dusting, and manipulating objects must be learned by young elephants. The amount of practice a young elephant needs to master the many uses of its extraordinary trunk is merely one dimension of the long period of learning elephants experience. It can be argued that the period of dependency for a young elephant is as long as that of a human child. Babies who are orphaned under the age of two do not survive their mother's death. Between the ages of two and five, up to 70% die in the two years following their mother's death, and between five and ten, 50% will die. Not only must survival and social techniques be learned but there is a strong emotional attachment between a calf and its mother. Anyone who has tried to raise an orphaned baby elephant will say that the first task is to help the calf overcome its grief.

Learning continues through the teenage years, and mothers have been observed leading their teenage daughters to the 'proper' mate, and guiding her through the steps of courtship. As with humans, teenagers do not usually make the best mothers (calf mortality is significantly higher among young mothers) and their offspring seem to know. Though they are suckled by their mothers, many babies of young mothers spend a large portion of their time with their grand-mothers.

The survival of females and their offspring depends upon the cohesion and co-ordination of the extended family, and on their ability to compete with other groups for access to scarce resources. It is not suprising, therefore, that these very social mammals have a large vocal repertoire. The vocal communcation of African elephants has been studied in more detail than that of Asian elephants. Family members use calls to reinforce bonds between relatives and friends, to care for youngsters, to reconcile differences between friends, to form coalitions against aggressors, and to keep in contact with one another over long distances.

African elephants emit a broad range of sounds, from low-frequency rumbles to higher-frequency trumpets, roars, screams, bellows, cries, gruffs, and snorts, as well as some idiosyncratic acoustic innovations. In all some 60 different calls are known. Many calls are typically emitted in chorus with other elephants. The rumbles are the most numerous (30 known) and complex class of calls. All of the rumbles contain components below the level of human hearing, with some being totally infrasonic.

Elephant rumbles are harmonic sounds, i.e. they contain frequencies that are multiples of the lowest or fundamental frequency. While the fundamental frequency is typically inaudiable to human ears, at least some of the upper

All family members help to take care of youngsters. This one-year-old baby has
raised his ears in alarm. His distress call would bring relatives, young and old, rushing to his
side with rumbles of reassurance and comforting touching with their trunks.

harmonics are usually within the audible range. Some calls are extraordinarily powerful and elephants can hear the lowest frequencies up to 6 miles (10 km) away. At dawn and dusk when atmospheric conditions are optimum calls can be heard over at least 110 square miles (285 sq km), but wind gusts and shimmering heat waves can break up sound waves and reduce that distance to less than a square mile. Elephants are also able to pick up these powerful signals through the ground over double these distances. Vibrations conducted through their skeletons may stimulate their very large middle-ear bones and, simultaneously, seismic vibrations may be detected via specialized motion-sensitive cells in their trunk and feet.

As a consequence of their highly social nature and their ability to communicate over long distances, elephants have an unusually extensive network of vocal recognition. It has been estimated that adult females are able to recognise the individual voices of at least 100 other adult females. While females use many different vocalisations in active communcation within and between family groups, males use many fewer calls, relying instead on listening to locate groups of females. Male elephants live a more solitary life, where reproductive success and survival depend to a degree upon an individual's ability to detect sounds made by others, and by advertising their sexual state, identify and rank.

If the only knowledge we had about elephants was tape recordings of their calls by sex and by age, we would immediately be struck by how apparently different the concerns of the two sexes are. Far from the supportive family life, adult males are on their own, living in a dynamic world where body size and condition, sexual state, dominance rank, and detailed knowledge of your rivals are what count. Male elephants leave their nurturing, closely bonded natal families at about 14 years old and must begin the task of learning a whole new set of rules that will then govern the rest of their lives. How do young males make this transition?

Sparring allows males to reassess the size and strength of their age mates.

Starting in the first year of life, male play is already noticeably rougher than that of females. By the age of four, when young females are helping to take care of younger babies, males are spending more time away from their mother's side, engaged in rough play with other young males. They are beginning the process of what will determine their success and even their survival as an adult: learning the characteristics of their age mates, and acquiring the ability to size up their rivals. From around the age of eight or nine years old males begin to spend some time away from the family, usually joining another family for a few days before returning. By an average age of 14 males have usually left their families.

At this young age they are still smaller than a fully grown adult female and less than half the weight of a large adult male. And, while they are growing, they still have much to learn. As the older males go about their business, searching for estrous females, mating and fighting, it is entertaining to observe teenage males tagging along behind, watching their mentors. In a subordinate, head low posture they will stand near or follow an older male, investigating each spot of urine that the older male has sniffed. The older males are gentle with these youngsters since, of course, at this age they pose no competition.

Male African elephants reach sexual maturity (that is the production of sperm in significant quantity) at about 17 years old. But at this age a young male is still only a little over half of his adult size, and cannot begin to compete with older males for access to mates. Although young males in their early twenties begin to try to mount estrous females, they are unlikely to be successful for several reasons. In natural populations there are many older, larger, more experienced males, and they work hard to ensure that younger males do not steal their mate. Even if they do have the opportunity to mate, the act itself takes a bit of practice. Unlike most other mammals, elephants have a highly mobile S-shaped penis and they do not thrust. It takes a young male a few years of practice to gain sufficient control over his penis to insert it successfully into

*In the first year of life a mother elephant keeps a very close watch on
her baby, waking him up when it is time to go, and checking that he is still behind her
by touching him gently with her hind foot and with a swish of her tail.*

Two musth males battle for supremacy.
Fights occur between musth males of equal fighting
ability and may end in injury or death.

a female's vagina. Once this has been achieved they have yet another major obstacle: females prefer to be mated by older males, and when mounted by a small male they simply take several steps forward, causing the male to fall off.

Once a male has reached his mid twenties he begins to show distinct sexually active and inactive periods. During sexually inactive periods males spend time alone or in small groups of other males in particular bull areas, where interactions are relaxed and amicable. During sexually active periods, males leave their bull areas and move in search of estrous females.

Then one day, during the height of a sexually active period, a male begins to exhibit a marked increase in aggression. His temporal glands, located behind his eyes, begin to secrete a viscous liquid, and urine begins to dribble from his penis. He has entered his first musth. The word musth comes from the Urdu, *mast*, meaning intoxicated in a sexual sense, and refers to a heightened period of sexual and aggressive activity, or rut. During musth, males secrete a viscous liquid from swollen temporal glands, leave a trail of strong smelling urine and call repeatedly in very low frequencies. Testosterone (the male hormone that controls sexual and aggressive behavior) rises dramatically above its non-musth level, and behavior becomes extremely aggressive toward other males, particularly toward those in musth.

Musth has been documented for centuries in domesticated Asian elephants because its occurrence caused such interruptions to the work schedule. Some of the historical documents written by the owners of working elephants are fascinating. Daily rationing of food and water was used to prevent the onset of musth, and if it was too late for prevention, remedies to minimize an elephant's rage included huge doses of Epsom salts or opium. In a book written in 1901 on the treatment of elephant diseases, G.H. Evans advised the following to calm a musth male's excitement:

> *Four to six drachmas of opium or ganja [marijuana] given with boiled rice, plantains or jaggery; or three drachmas of camphor and two of*

opium twice a day for two days; or eight pounds each of wheat flour, onions, and sugar and four pounds of ghee [clarified butter], mixed together and worked into orange-sized pills and administered one each night and morning until the whole is taken.

According to Evans, after this treatment most animals would carry on their work as usual.

For many years it was believed that musth did not occur in African elephants, and it was less than 20 years ago that it was first documented in the African genus. It is ironic that today more is known about the phenomenon among free living elephants in Africa than in Asia. Musth appears to be almost identical in the two genera, and the only significant difference seems to be that Asian elephants come into musth at a slightly younger age. Most of these cases, however, occur in captivity where there is little or no suppression of musth by the presence of older, larger males. Among wild African elephants the occurrence of musth in younger males is strongly influenced by the proximity of older musth males. For example, a young male may come into musth within an hour of encountering an unguarded estrous female, but be forced out of musth immediately following an attack by a higher ranking musth male.

Among young males the duration of musth is short and sporadic, while the musth periods of older males last several months and occur at a predictable time each year. The highest ranking males in a population come into musth during and following the rains when females are in bigger groups and the greatest number are likely to come into estrous. As a consequence of continued growth in height and body weight, larger, older males rank above smaller, younger males and thus male elephants do not reach their sexual prime until they are 45 years old. These older males are successful not only because of their large size, but because females actively choose to mate with them.

Elephants enjoy water from a very young age.

Elephants and Humans

The relationship between elephants and man is and has been an extraordinary one. We view elephants with a degree of respect and fondness that we reserve for few other creatures on earth. And yet, however much our affinity for elephants, our relationship with them has always been an exploitative one. Elephants have been hunted for meat and for ivory, killed for raiding our crops, captured for domestication, trained for carrying out tasks and for performing in circuses or religious ceremonies.

Elephants were first tamed in the Indus Valley about 2000 BC and were used for a range of chores. Today there are about 15,000 working elephants in Asia, making up more than a third of the entire Asian elephant population. Elephants are employed to carry tourists in national parks, to haul loads, to pull logs out of forests, to capture wild elephants, to lead religious ceremonies and to assist in many other activities that require strength and intelligence. The qualities said to make elephants so useful, in comparison with machinery, include their intelligence, flexibility (they can work almost anywhere from in water to dense forest, to steep hillsides), low maintenance costs, and minimal impact on the environment. It is common for elephants to know over 30 commands although, apparently, they don't always wait to be told. They seem to understand what is expected of them and if something is out of place they will often rectify it of their own volition. Many people who work with elephants argue that they have reasoned thought. For example, domesticated elephants have been known to stuff mud into the bells around their necks to muffle them before they go out into the neighboring farms to steal bananas.

Elephants have also been used in war, and the first record of an elephant killed in battle dates back to 1100 BC in the Indus Valley. Elephants were

An Asian elephant is given a daily bath by her mahout.

trained either to pass the enemy up to their mahouts, who would dispatch him, or to hold the enemy down with the trunk or foreleg while impaling him with a tusk. Porus, Emperor of India, used 85 elephants to confront Alexander the Great at the Battle of Hydaspes in 326 BC. And Ptolemy, one of Alexander's generals, imported Indian elephants to Egypt. African elephants, too, were used in battle and when Ptolemy's elephants aged and died, his son, Ptolemy II, ensured a steady supply by capturing wild African elephants. The use of war elephants spread across North Africa and into the peninsula of Greece where in 280 BC King Pyrrhus invaded Italy with 20 elephants, causing the Roman horses to panic. Hannibal transported a corps of 37 African elephants through southern Spain and France and across the Alps to invade Italy in 218 BC. Though his invasion was daringly conceived and brilliantly executed most of his elephants eventually succumbed to disease.

In modern times, too, African elephants have been trained. In 1879 the Belgian king, Leopold II, attempted to bring four Asian elephants to the Congo but all died on the way. Twenty years later he attempted to catch wild African elephant calves by first shooting the mother and then sending men running after the frightened calf, looping one end of a rope around its leg and the other end around a tree. By 1913 there were 33 elephants in captivity at the Elephant Domestication Center, and the elephants were eventually trained to work in agriculture and forestry. The Center still exists today in the Garamba National Park in the Democratic Republic of Congo (formerly Zaire), where elephants are used for taking tourists on game rides. Elephant-back safaris are also available in the Okavango Delta, Botswana, and a number of other elephant safari centers are starting up around the continent.

Sadly the most common interaction between man and elephants today is one of conflict. There are simply too many people and expanding agriculture is encroaching on most elephant habitats. The single biggest threat to the future survival of elephants is the shrinking habitat available to them. Within

our own recorded history elephants formed an almost continuous series of populations from Africa to China. We have whittled them down to two main groups, African and Asian elephants, which are now separated by several thousand miles.

Asian elephants were once distributed from Syria and Iraq to China and south to Sumatra. Throughout history Asian elephants have disappeared where forests have been cleared for human needs. Today their distribution is very fragmented and elephants occur only in small populations in India, Sri Lanka, Nepal, Bhutan, Bangladesh, Myanmar (formerly Burma), China, Thailand, Laos, Cambodia, Vietnam, Malaysia and Indonesia. The total Asian elephant population is estimated at fewer than 44,000 individuals, and loss of habitat and poaching are the cause of the elephants' declining numbers and endangered status. Exploding human populations have turned crucial elephant habitats into farmland and eliminated traditional migratory routes; slash and burn agriculture has destroyed large sections of forest, fragmenting populations and making the long-term survival of elephants in many areas unlikely. As agriculture expands and elephant habitat shrinks, conflict between people and elephants can only increase. In India alone between 200 and 300 people are killed by elephants each year. In most countries there is little future for the Asian elephant except in a few protected areas.

Ancient historical writings document the occurrence of African elephants in North Africa as far as the Mediterranean coast. And, within the last five decades, African elephants inhabited all sub-Saharan Africa except for extremely arid areas. Today, though elephants still exist in 34 African countries, their range is fragmented and populations are becoming increasingly isolated.

While habitat loss has primarily accounted for the recent decrease in Asian elephant numbers, the quest for ivory can be held responsible for the decline of

There is so little space left for elephants.

Between 1979 and 1989 over half a million African elephants were illegally killed to meet the world's demand for ivory. In 1989 Kenya burned its ivory stockpile in a clear statement that the trade should be banned; it was, later that year, with dramatic and positive results. The 1997 decision to reopen a limited trade in ivory sends a mistaken green light to consumers, and an ominous message to elephants. Mutilated carcasses may once again become a common sight in Africa's national parks.

the African elephant. Ivory is a beautiful substance, coveted by humans for at least the last 25,000 years. The oldest ivory sculpture, the *Venus of Landes*, was found in a cave in France, and dates from the Upper Palaeolithic. All the great ancient civilizations of Asia, Europe and Africa prized elephant ivory, and ivory carving centers dating from before 3000 BC have been uncovered in Babylon.

The demand for ivory has continued throughout human history, and indications are that it was primarily pressure from ivory hunting which caused the extinction of elephants in North Africa in the Middle Ages. Excessive hunting in the eighteenth and nineteenth centuries brought elephants in southern Africa to the brink of extinction, and a similar rush for ivory took place in West Africa, peaking in the nineteenth and early twentieth centuries, from which populations have never recovered. The rapid decline of the elephants across sub-Saharan Africa during the eighteenth and nineteenth centuries was closely linked with the slave trade, as slave caravans were used to transport tusk to the coast from the interior.

The message: do not sell, buy, or wear ivory.

Protective legislation and a fall in the price of ivory during the first three-quarters of this century allowed many populations to recover. But by the 1970s the killing of elephants for ivory was, once again, having a serious impact on populations across most of the African continent. The paradox was that while elephants were undergoing a significant continental decline, certain populations within protected areas were locally overabundant and judged in need of culling. Many people argued that if elephants were to be legally killed then ivory should be legally traded. The problem was that by the mid 1980s, 80% of the tusks in trade were actually from illegally killed elephants. In 1979 the continental population estimate was 1.3 million elephants, and by 1989 the figure was 609,000; over half of Africa's elephants had been killed during the decade. Finally, in 1989, based on these and other alarming statistics, the Convention on International Trade in Endangered Species (CITES) banned the international trade in ivory. The effect of the ivory trade ban was an immediate drop in the price of ivory across most of Africa and a dramatic decline in the level of poaching. Since then the ban on the trade has been relaxed in a few countries and the consequences of this decision are still being debated.

Unfortunately, ivory poaching is but one of the problems threatening the survival of the African elephant. In most areas where they now live human populations are growing at rates of between 3% and 4% per annum. Traditional elephant habitat is being carved up for agriculture and elephants are increasingly being confined in parks and reserves, which are often too small to support them year round. As individuals try to move beyond their boundaries they meet opposition from farmers. A common solution is to fence most elephants inside protected areas, and to shoot any that come into conflict with people outside. But in many places land-hungry people are encroaching upon the protected forests, parks and reserves that have been set aside for elephants.

The earth's elephants are under threat and although our generation will not witness the last of these extraordinary creatures, ours may be the generation that decides their fate. Will we stand by and watch as the remaining elephants are killed by ivory poachers, shot for raiding crops, or fenced into small protected areas to be culled on a regular basis? Or will we have the imagination and the courage to find a better way to live with elephants?

What will their future be?

African Elephant Facts

Scientific name	*Loxodonta africana*	Interbirth interval	4–6 years
Ave. max height (male)	almost 13 ft (4 m)	Age at first musth	average 29 years
		Longevity	60–70 years
Ave. max height (female)	just under 9 ft (2.7 m)	Skin	wrinkled
		Shape of back	concave
Ave. max weight (male)	over 13,200 lb (6000 kg)	Teeth	lozenge-shaped loops
Ave. max weight (female)	6100 lb (2767 kg)	Tusks	both sexes
Ave. weight newborn	265 lb (120 kg)	Tip of trunk	two finger
Age at first reproduction	8–18 years	Ave. max tusk weight (male)	108 lb (49 kg)
Gestation	660 days	Ave. max tusk weight (female)	15 lb (7 kg)

Asian Elephant Facts

Scientific name	*Elephas maximus*	Longevity	60–70 years
Ave. max height (male)	up to 11.5 ft (3.5 m)	Skin	smoother
		Shape of back	convex
Ave. max weight (male)	up to 12,125 lb (5500 kg)	Teeth	narrow compressed loops
Ave. weight newborn	165–253 lb (75–115 kg)	Tusks	females tuskless
Age at first reproduction	8–13 years	Tip of trunk	one finger
		Ave. max tusk weight (female)	usually vestigial or absent
Gestation	about 660 days		
Interbirth interval	4–6 years		

Index

Recommended Reading

Chadwick, D, *The Fate of the Elephant*, London, 1993.
Douglas-Hamilton, I & O., *Battle for the Elephants*, London, 1992.
Moss, C. J. *Elephant Memories*, New York, 1988.
Poole, Joyce, J. *Coming of Age with Elephants*, New York, 1996.
Shoshani, J. *Elephants: Majestic Creatures of the Wild*, Sydney, 1992.
Sukumar, R. *The Living Elephants: Evolutionary Ecology, Behavior, and Conservation*, Oxford, 2003.

The Author

Joyce Poole received her Ph.D in animal behavior from Cambridge University and completed her post-doctoral training at Princeton University. She has spent over 20 years studying the elephants of Amboseli National Park, her research there focusing on the sexual and aggressive behavior of musth males and on vocal communication. In the early 1990s Joyce headed Kenya's elephant conservation and management program.